Basics – Theory for Scuba Divers

- A related to practice textbook -

With practical exercises via QR-Code

Basic Diver

Junior Open Water Diver

Open Water Diver

Diver *

and Nitrox 1

Basics – Theory for Scuba Divers

Author Karsten Reimer

FSC
www.fsc.org
MIX
Papier aus ver-
antwortungsvollen
Quellen
Paper from
responsible sources
FSC® C105338

Bibliographic Information of the German National library:

The German National library listed this publication in the German in the German
National bibliography; detailed bibliographic data are available on the internet via
http://dnb.dnb.de

1. Edition (English) December 2019

All Illustrations are from the actual teaching material of the International Diving
Association - IDA GbR - and with friendly approval of the corresponding
companies and right holders.

Karsten Reimer

Author

Production and publishing:

BoD – Books on Demand, Norderstedt, Germany

ISBN 9783734729423

Foreword

This book does not replace a comprehensive dive theory textbook, but is a guide to gaining the theoretical knowledge necessary to pass the exams for the dive courses listed on the front page. So to speak "dive theory without ballast"! For those who want to delve deeper into the subject, the market offers many good and much more comprehensive textbooks. This book is based on the timing of a dive training; that means it starts with the introductory dive and then builds on the acquired knowledge. In this book, the male salutation is used to simplify the writing. Of course that does not mean that only men should dive. There are even voices in the "diving scene" claiming that women are the better divers. In view of the often irresponsible willingness to take risks of my male contemporaries, this is a thesis that I would definitely subscribe to.

Even though ☺

Divers are men who can live and work under water or in non-respirable air.
Divers are men of great muscle power, with healthy organs. There is no second profession that places as high demands on physical performance as the profession of the diver requires, not just occasionally. Wearing the almost 100 kg heavy armor outside the water, or the movement of this mass while walking under water, breathing under rapidly changing pressure and, not least, most strenuous work under not always perfect air supply, require athletic muscles, healthy lungs, strong heart and proper functioning of all organs. Divers are men of high spiritual powers, of intellect and impeccable morality. They have to defy such diverse dangers that the highest demands are placed on their presence of mind and observation. To do useful and fast diving work is at the same time the actual art of the diver, which makes his activity valuable. An unflinching sense of duty must drive him to provide the fastest and most effective solution to the task by giving all the powers of his body and mind.

Manual for divers
Hermann Stelzner
Director and Chief engineer of the Drägerwerk
*Lübeck **1931***

It may have been like that in 1931. Today, diving is possible for anyone. However, health is still an important requirement.

Content

1. The entry or important for your Discover Scuba course!

Page

1.1	The diving mask – See and hear under water	1
1.2	The snorkel – pendulum breathing and Lung vacuum barotrauma	8
1.3	The fins – swimming style	14
1.4	The pressure equalization	17
1.5	The ear	21
1.6	The Regulator – breathing under water	24
1.7	Buoyancy and rescue Jacket - buoyancy	29
1.8	The tank	31
1.9	The wet suit - Insolation - Archimedes	33
1.10	The weights	37
1.11	The Sign language	40
1.12	Tips for your Discover SCUBA course	50

2. Additional equipment

2.1	The divers knife – a tool, no weapon -	51
2.2	The divers watch	53
2.3	The depth gauge	55
2.4	The divers computer	58
2.5	The divers flag	60
2.6	The compass	62
2.7	The divers torch	64
2.8	Safety equipment	65
2.9	More about the tank	68
2.10	More about the regulator	73

3. Diving medicine

3.1	The barotrauma	77
3.2	The breathing and essouflement	80
3.3	The depth intoxication	85
3.4	Hyperventilation – pool- und shallow water unconsciousness	86
3.5	The diving reflexes – water-nose-reflex	89
3.6	The decompression sickness	91
3.7	The rescue chain	98
3.8	Hypo- und hyperthermia	106
3.9	Diving and nutrition	109

3.10	Diving and drugs	110

4.   Diving physics

4.1	The law of Henry	111
4.2	The law of Archimedes	113
4.3	The law of Boyle & Mariotte	113
4.4	The law of Gay Lussac	115
4.5	The law of Dalton	117

5.   Diving practice

5.1	General rules	121
5.2	The briefing	124
5.3	The partner check	126
5.4	Environmentally friendly behavior	130
5.5	The dive calculation	132
5.6	The use of the decompression table	139
5.7	Notes for altitude diving / mountain lakes	145
5.8	Notes for diving before or after flying	146
5.9	Emergency card	147
6.0	**Diving with Nitrox**	150
7.0	Appendix and glossary	188/189
	Statement of health	193
	Notes	198

1. The entry or important for your Discover Scuba course!

To show the beginner wether diving is the right sport for him, it is a good idea to start with a „Discover Scuba course"! There you can check if it is the right sport before you sign in to a complete diving course. The physical suitability for the diving sport, which is best proved by a medical certificate of a specialized divers doctor, must not be forgotten either. Your instructor has the right forms for you. If you do not feel well underwater, you should look for another hobby. As hard as it may be.

The ABC equipment (1.1 to 1.3)

In former times the graders are used to need a blackboard, a piece of chalk and a sponge to learn writing and arithmetic. This was the equipment for the „ABC graders", and this is what the snorkle diver's equipment is also called.

1.1 The diving mask

Rim, double or single seal (single seal, mostly only under the nose)

Mask body, silicon or rubber   **Mask frame,** plastic or (seldom) metal

Buckle, to adjust

the mask strap   T

Nose pocket

Safety glasses (Tempered glass)

We need the mask to see clear and sharp under water. The smaller the internal volume of the mask (so called „dead space") is the easier it is to clear the mask from penetrated water and the wider the angle of view.

When purchasing your mask, make sure that you can grip your nose well with your thumb and forefinger to make pressure equalization (see page 19) (**Nosepocket**). A diving mask consists of the **glasses** (for a lot of masks you can buy optical lenses), the **mask body**, made of silicon or rubber und **the frame**, mostly made of plastic. Masks with additional extensions like valves or snorkels are not recommended and sometimes even dangerous. The mask strap is mostly made of the same material as the mask, silicon or rubber. The individual length of the mask strap will be customized to the head size. This is done by adjusting the two buckles left and right on the frame. Since you usually only adjust the mask band once for yourself, the stable seat is more important than a particularly simple adjustment. Also make sure that the mask glass has a print that shows it is a safety glass. („T" or Tempered glass or safety glass). Window glass is unsuitable and can lead to loss of sight if it is damaged. When buying, you should prefer masks made of silicone, because the material is anti-allergic and very UV-stable. A browning of the silicone over the years is harmless. In addition, masks made of rubber are extremely sensitive to suncream, which you should wash from your face anyway before each dive. An absolutely leakproof mask does not exist because there's no face with the absolute perfect fit. That means that there's mostly always a little bit of water in your mask. If this water mixes with your sweat and / or suncream, it will result in a "lotion", which burns your eyes worse than any water is able to. To prevent fogging of the mask glass, there are various remedies to buy in the market; but you always have the simplest and "cheapest" anti-fogging agent: your saliva. Spit inside once on each glass and rub the saliva well on the glass. Then rinse the mask briefly in the water and thats all. With new masks, a lubricant film made of silicone oil is often found on the glasses due to the manufacturing process. It must be removed, otherwise the mask will fog permanently, no matter how often you spit into it. To remove this lubricating film, every diver has his own home remedies. I have good experience with liquid silicone remover from the hardware store, but it should also work with toothpaste or Coca Cola. Also the flame of a lighter should work, but since the mask can take damage, you should not try this. Rinse your mask after each dive with fresh water and store the mask cool, dark and dry, then you enjoy it for a long time. Buy your mask in a diving shop or ask the instructor of your confidence to help. A diving specialist dealer or a well-trained instructor knows exactly what you need and you also have a direct contact person for questions about the product.

Dead space of the mask (internal volume)

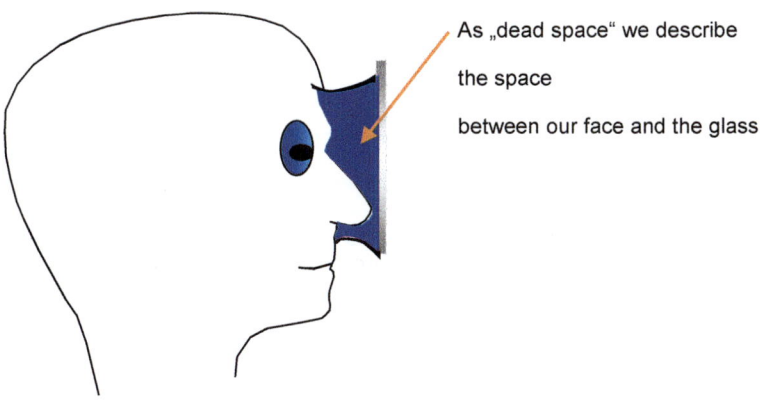

As „dead space" we describe the space

between our face and the glass.

We have to clear this "dead space" from penetrated water by exhaling out of the nose and pressing the upper rim to the forehead.

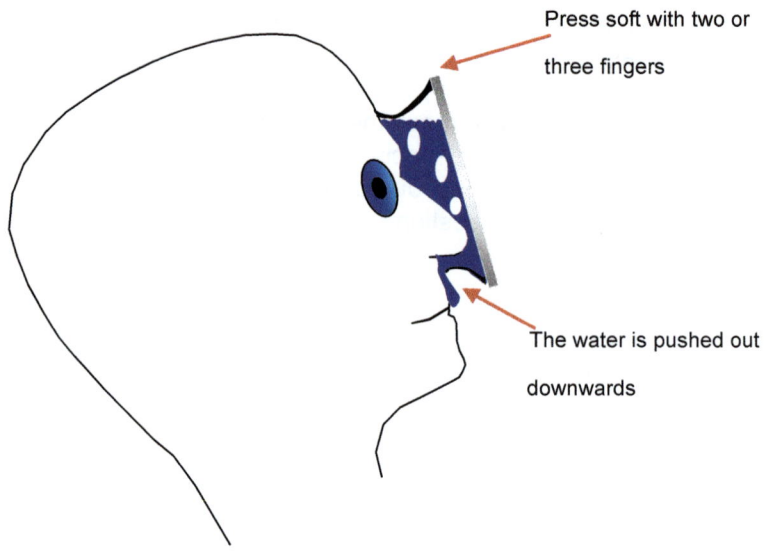

Press soft with two or three fingers

The water is pushed out downwards

For this purpose, we tilt our head slightly backwards, press the upper edge of the mask lightly against the forehead and exhale slowly and continuously through the nose. The water in the mask is now forced downwards out of the mask by the exhaled air. This exercise is a pure diligence exercise and does not necessarily succeed the first time. But practice also makes the master here. I promise you that there are many dives in your life, after which you cannot even say if and how often you have cleared the mask during the dive, that's because it becomes routine over time. There is not a "too much" air blown in as the surplus air escapes through the seals of the mask and the mask gently lays on your face again. This ensures that the internal pressure of the mask is equal to the external pressure. Then you have a clear view again.

If you want, you can also have a look at the exercise if you have a QR code reader installed on your mobile. You can get this app for free via the Google Shop or in the Apple App Store. Using IOS, you only need to open the camera app and point the lens at the QR code. I would like to point out that these are photos that were taken in summer in the Baltic Sea near Kiel and therefore, due to the increased algae growth, is to be expected with sometimes poor visibility. But the diving does not always take place in the pool or in the crystal clear water. Naturally, it is not necessary to "clear" the hood in order to restore tightness if the mask has not been removed completely, as in the film.

Seeing under water

1/3 bigger and 1/4 nearer

Which brings us to "seeing"! Seeing under water is not the same as seeing over water. Apart from the fact that the visibility under water is usually not as good as in air anyway, as there are always suspended solids in the water, which affect the clarity of the water. Due to the seasonal algae bloom or whirled up sediment (sand or similar), the visibility may deteriorate considerably. Due to the different refractive indices of air and water (1: 1.33), we see everything under water 1/3 larger and 1/4 closer than it actually is. Just take it as nature has given, when diving itself has almost no influence. There is even more influence of the water's ability to filter out the light of its wavelength.

Colors under water

In the order **red, orange, yellow, green, blue and purple** the colors are no longer perceived with increasing depth, because the "white" light of the surface, which is composed of the individual spectral colors of the light, is filtered out on the way in the depth according to the wavelength of the individual colors. In practice, this means that the colors (reds and yellows), which still have signal effect on the water surface, lose their signal effect under water after a few meters. In order to be able to recognize the colors then, all you need is a diving torch, which contains all the spectral colors with its white light. Illuminate the objects and then everything is back in color as usual. This feature of the water is also the reason why when photographing or filming under water necessarily a corresponding lighting should be used. Thus, according to the following drawing, the colors are so strongly deprived of water already at the specified depths, that they can no longer be clearly identified. From about 60 meters, all colors are filtered out so far that a recognition of the color blue is no longer possible.

Sequence of color absorption in the water!

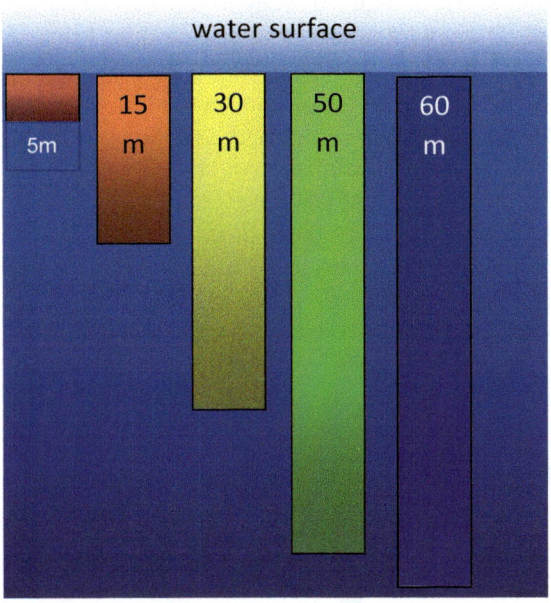

Hearing under water

Even underwater listening is different to listening in the air. The sound, that is the noise, spreads over water at a speed of about **340 meters per second**. The denser the medium in which the sound is transmitted, the higher the speed of sound. In the water, we expect a speed of sound of about 1480 meters per second. So the sound spreads under water about 4.3 times as fast as in the air. Since our hearing system is designed for the speed of sound in the air, we cannot pinpoint a potential sound source, a boat or a dive partner who wants to attract attention underwater. We hear the sound, but we do not know exactly where it comes from.

Noise, which is produced above the water surface, is barely noticeable under water, as the water surface reflects a large part of the sound. However, we perceive the engine noise of boats as very loud, as this sound is transmitted directly to the surrounding water via the boat hull. Thus, with noises that could come from boats or ships, only emerge when an endangering is no longer given. Keep in mind that the engine noise can be quieter even if the operator only reduces the engine speed. Of course, you must also pay attention to watercraft that make no or little noise, such as sailboats, surfers or rowboats. It is still safest if you emerge in the immediate vicinity of buoys, bridge piers or anchored watercraft. Make sure you pay attention to a possibly rotating propeller. Injuries that you can get when touching a rotating propeller are very serious.

1.2 The snorkel

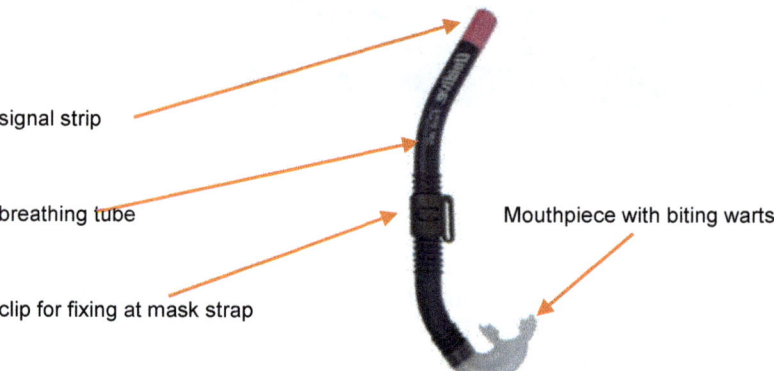

signal strip

breathing tube

Mouthpiece with biting warts

clip for fixing at mask strap

The snorkel is a tube that moves our breathing opening, in this case the mouth, to the back of the head, so that we can lay relaxed on the water surface and can study the fish. Normally we breathe through the nose, but as we use a diving mask to be able to see underwater, this breathing opening is denied us when diving.

What applies to the mask, also applies to the snorkel, if possible without any attachments. It consists of a rubber or plastic tube, a mouthpiece with biting warts (mostly silicone), a rubber or a clip to attach it to the mask strap (not essential, can also be put under the mask strap) and the signal strip at the top of the snorkel (should be signal red to signal to other water sportsmen that someone is snorkeling here). Some snorkels today have a valve at the bottom of the arch. This should drain the water to the water level and make it easier to blow it out (works very well in most cases), but represents a possible source of error if the valve does not close properly due to pollution, so a "matter of taste". **The snorkel for adults should never be longer than 35 cm and the inside diameter must not exceed 25 mm; for children, the dimensions are 30 cm in length and 18 mm in diameter.** An extension of the snorkel and / or an increase of the inner diameter has serious health consequences. If we extend the snorkel or use a longer tube to "snorkel deeper", we can harm our body massively and even die.

We can safely assume that a snorkeler who floats on the water surface is quite relaxed at this moment. Through this relaxation, he breathes little and not very deep in and out. We are talking about a minute ventilation (BMV), which describes the amount of air in liters that "consumes" a diver per minute. Where "consumed" does not really hit the core, but we'll come to that later on. Each breath requires about 0.5 liters of air at rest. Our breathing air is a gas mixture, consisting of nitrogen (78%), oxygen (21%) and the residual gases (1% carbon dioxide, noble gases and moisture). All we really need is oxygen, but under normal circumstances we do not have a choice. Let us assume that such a snorkel has an internal volume, depending on the length and the diameter of about 0.2 liters. These 0.2 liters are the so-called dead space of the snorkel, so the volume that does not actively participate in the breathing, but this volume we must consider. Humans themselves have already integrated a natural volume of dead space in the airways, namely the bronchi, the trachea and the nasopharynx. These components of the respiratory tract are not compressible, so they are only passively flushed by our breathing air, as well as the dead space of the snorkel.

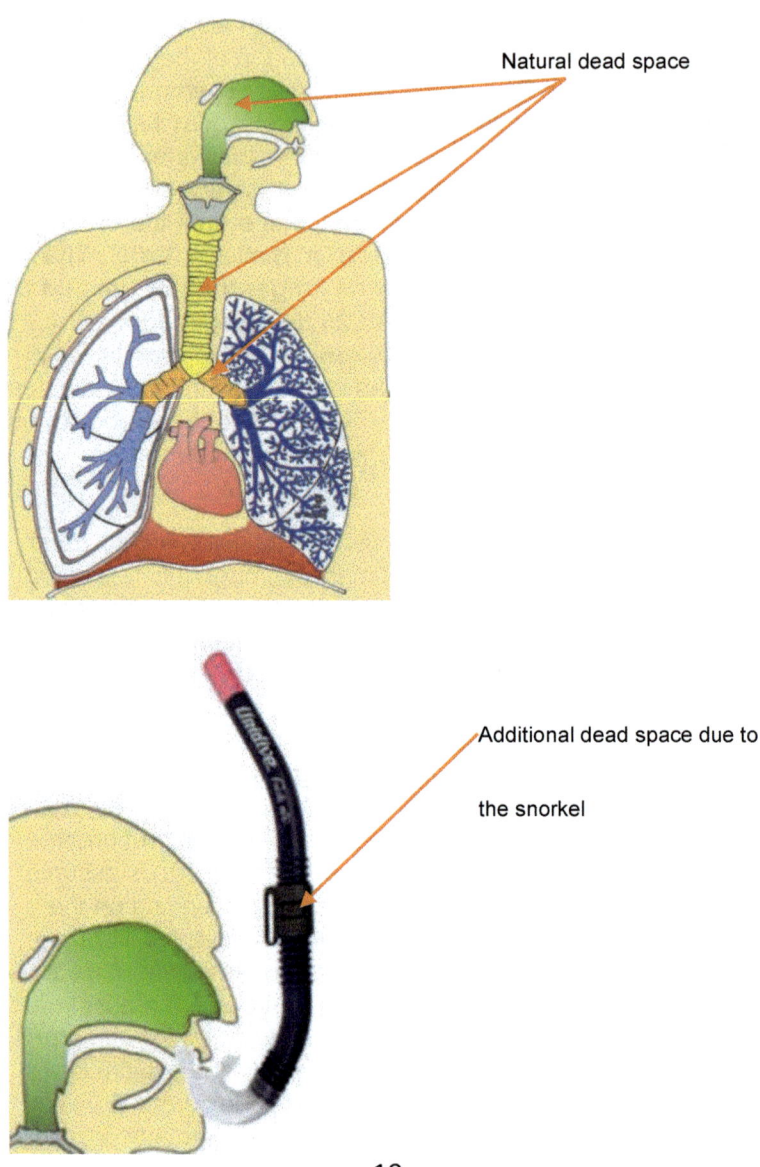

Natural dead space

Additional dead space due to

the snorkel

10

This natural dead space (oral cavity, nasopharynx, trachea and bronchi) is assumed to be approx. 0.15 liters in adults. If we breathe in and out about 0.5 liter at rest, we have 0.2 liters of exhaled air in our snorkel. Our exhaled air has an oxygen content of about 17% as our body converts 4% to carbon dioxide. This means that with the next breath we already breathe in a lower oxygen content than with the first breath. Thus, the oxygen content in our inhaled air continuously drops, and just as with yawning, the body gains the oxygen it needs through occasional deeper breaths. However, if our snorkel is so bulky in diameter and / or length that we breathe in almost all of our exhaled air again, there is a relatively short supply of oxygen to the brain and the risk of fainting increases rapidly. And those who pass out in the water either have an attentive partner by their side or are quite unlucky.

This breathing in and out of used air is called pendulum or dead space breathing and this is absolutely to be avoided.

The second dangerous aspect, the too great length of the snorkel, is also to be considered, even if this aspect is more of a hypothetical nature: for anyone who has ever attempted to breathe through a garden hose has usually been cured. Again, assume that the snorkeler has extended his snorkel to one meter to get closer to the fish. Quite apart from the fact that the snorkeler will now have great problems without a weight belt and with (still) filled lung in one meter of water depth. Now it's getting physically. **The air pressure at the sea surface is according to physical definition 101325 Pa = 101.325 kPa = 1013.25 hPa ≈ 1 bar.**

Pa stands for Pascal and is a unit of pressure, named after the French scientist Blaise Pascal. A Pascal is the force that a Newton exerts over an area of one square meter. Ten Newton is the force that causes about 1 kilogram. Do not worry, it will not get worse, but you need to know how the different pressures affect your body. Namely the normal atmospheric pressure and the newly added hydrostatic pressure, the pressure exerted by the water.

Atmospheric pressure (air pressure)

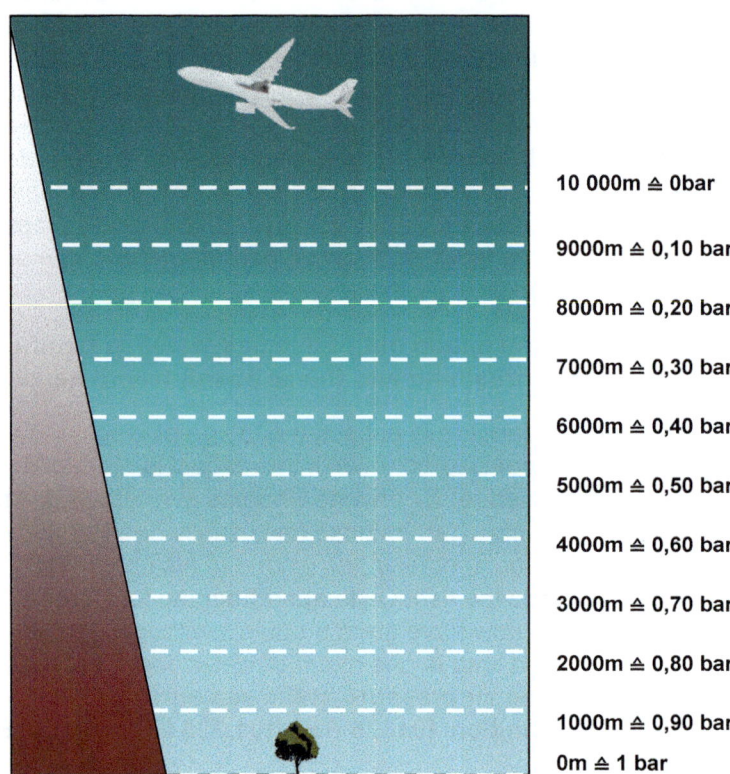

10 000m ≙ 0bar

9000m ≙ 0,10 bar

8000m ≙ 0,20 bar

7000m ≙ 0,30 bar

6000m ≙ 0,40 bar

5000m ≙ 0,50 bar

4000m ≙ 0,60 bar

3000m ≙ 0,70 bar

2000m ≙ 0,80 bar

1000m ≙ 0,90 bar

0m ≙ 1 bar

One liter of air weighs 1.29 grams, so it is not, as often assumed, without weight. The total amount of air, that is the so-called atmosphere that weighs on us, exerts a pressure of about 1.0 bar at sea level, which results from the fact that the air, as well as everything else that is on it, is attracted from the Earth. As the

12

altitude increases, less air is put on us, which means that the pressure on us is reduced. And per 1000 meters height by 0.1 bar, as can be seen from the outline above.

However, water is much heavier than air and we expect 1.0 kg (kilograms) per liter for fresh water and 1.03 kg for one liter of salt water. The higher weight of salt water results from the dissolved minerals that are missing the fresh water.

Hydrostatic pressure (water pressure)

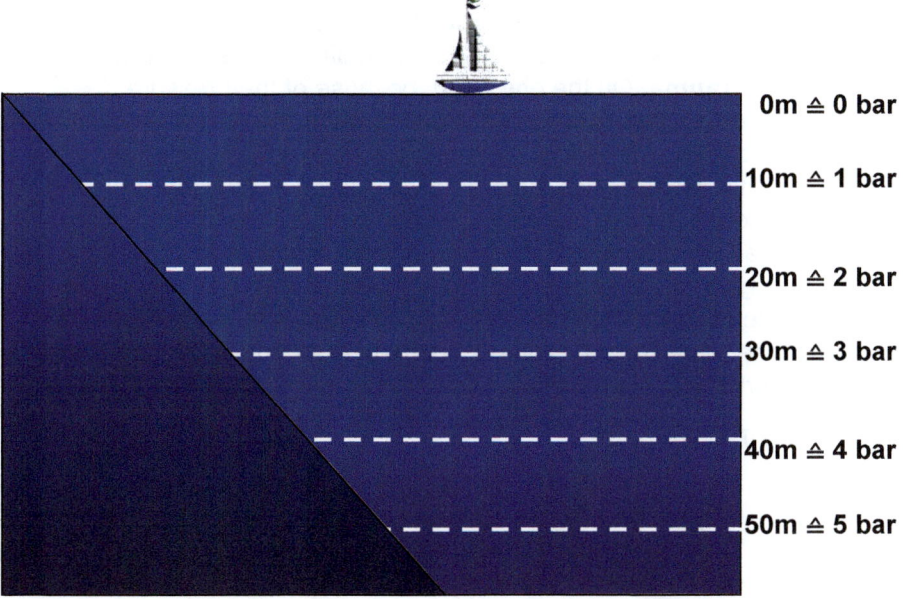

Water has a weight and we assume that, as already mentioned, in fresh water of a weight of 1.0 kg per liter and in salt water of 1.03 kg per liter. In practice, this means that the amount of water that is lying above us and thus weighs on us with increasing depth is getting more and more and thus exerts a steadily increasing pressure on us. Since we are or want to be divers and not meteorologists or physicists, we use the common unit bar for all our calculations. In one meter of water, we have an ambient

13

pressure of 1.1 bar. At the water surface we have an ambient pressure of 1.0 bar. Thus, there is a pressure difference of 0.1 bar. Sounds like little, but has consequences. While the 1.1 bar weighs on our body, the interior of our lungs is connected via the snorkel tube with the surface pressure of 1.0 bar. Thus, our respiratory muscles (diaphragm and rib muscles) must work against this pressure difference, which quickly leads to fatigue of these muscles. Due to the relative negative pressure that now exists in the lungs, it is almost impossible to inhale air and tissue fluid will increasingly enter the lungs. This is an attempt by the body to compensate the negative pressure. The general term for such processes, caused by pressure differences, is called **barotrauma**. On the one hand, because of the pressure difference, we have problems filling the lungs with fresh air at all, but on the other hand, the body is also working against us, as it additionally reduces the breathable surface of the lungs by the leaked tissue fluid. Thus, there is a lack of oxygen and severe breathing problems, which announce by shortness of breath and cough and can end with a fainting. This form of barotrauma is called lung vacuum barotrauma / lung negative barotrauma or "inner blue coming" and occurs mainly during free diving. And of course with snorkelers whose snorkel cannot be long enough.

1.3 The fins

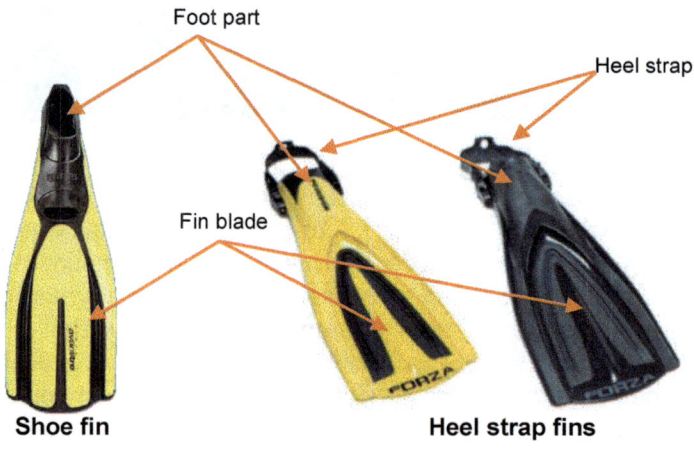

Foot part

Heel strap

Fin blade

Shoe fin **Heel strap fins**

14

Generally, there are two different "types" of fins. The "design" of a fin also determines its name. We distinguish between shoe and heel strap fin. The shoe fin is also often called a swimming pool fin and the heel strap fin is also called scuba fin. Although both fin types are suitable for both applications, they are not optimal for each use. For any of these two categories, there are countless types of construction which differ by tunnels, channels, flaps or other optimizations. For the beginner, it is only important that the fin fits well, does not press, does not slip on the foot and has a degree of firmness of the fin leaf that corresponds to the student's level of training.

An inexperienced fin swimmer should tend to a soft rather than a hard fin leaf. A hard fin leaf unnecessarily stresses the joints, muscles, and ligaments of leg and foot, and may cause pain and even damage. The soft fin blade has unfortunately also disadvantages, for example when swimming against strong current or when trying to get into the dinghy. But since the beginner is always accompanied by his instructor, the dive guide, the instructor assistant or experienced divers, this problem is negligible for now. The shoe fin, often called swimming fin, has a molded foot part, which forms a unit with the fin blade. This fin is adjusted similarly to the shoe on the surface of the individual foot size. This type of fin is primarily used in warm waters and is good for snorkeling or swimming, but is also used for diving with the SCUBA (**S**elf **c**ontained **u**nderwater **b**reathing **a**pparatus). The heel strap fin has no molded foot part but only an opening that holds the front part of the foot. The heel is then pressed firmly into the foot part of the fin by means of a heel band or a so-called springstrap (a steel spring, similar to the pen of a ballpoint pen, only larger and rustproof).

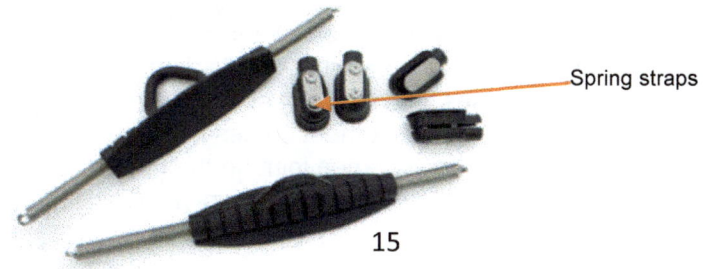

Spring straps

15

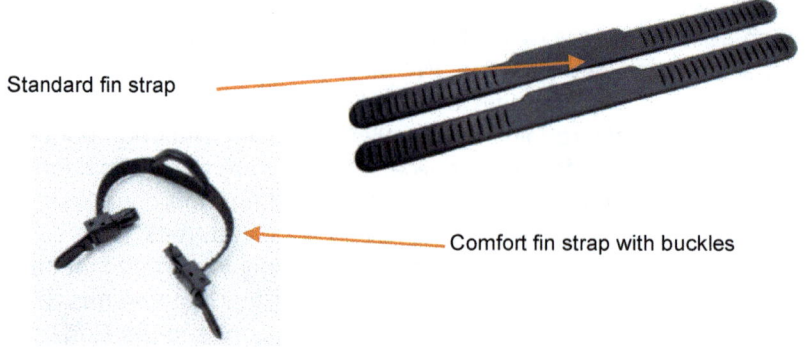

Standard fin strap

Comfort fin strap with buckles

If you have carefully read the last sentence, you will realize that these fins are not comfortable for divers who are barefooted. Therefore, the heel strap fin is (almost) used exclusively by scuba divers who wear a shoe made of neoprene, the so-called foot let. We will come to foot let and neoprene later. These heel strap fins, since they are designed for scuba divers, are usually more stable and heavier than the shoe fin. Also, the fin blade is often wider and harder, so that a scuba diver, which brings due to its equipment significantly more mass on the scales, can assert itself against currents better. Provided the general constitution of the diver plays along with it. Which brings us to the swimming style. Fins should never be worn on land walking into the water. If you have to walk with them in the water walk backwards. If you prefer to make your own experience, you are welcome to go for a walk on the beach, but please with **your own fins**. Apart from the fact that this is very uncomfortable and looks silly, the owner of the fins will quickly find out that the two edges left and right of the fin blade, like to quit this type of movement with breaking.

The fins are generally attached just before jumping into the water or in the water. The same applies while leaving the water. Finally, fish only carry their fins in the water. Okay, the comparison is limp, but leads us directly to the swimming style. In the water, we use our fins as the fish uses its fins. Calm and uniform and in harmony with the water. The movement comes from the hip and neither from the foot nor from the knee joint. In the upward stroke the knee remains almost unbowed, on the down stroke it is

16

slightly bent. So, according to the swimming style of the fish, a wave motion is intended, neither a "cycling" nor a dog "paddling". Practice is necessary and your instructor will tell you if it is good or needs improvement. Remember, the water is always "stronger" and it works only with the water, but never against the water. So stay relaxed.

1.4 Pressure equalization

In our body there are several cavities, which are lined by strongly perfused mucous membrane and which are filled with our breathing air. This is in addition to our lungs, the entire nasopharynx and various "cavities" within the head: ethmoidal cells, sphenoid sinus, mastoid cells, middle ear, frontal sinuses and maxillary sinuses. You do not have to remember these names, but you should know their existence.

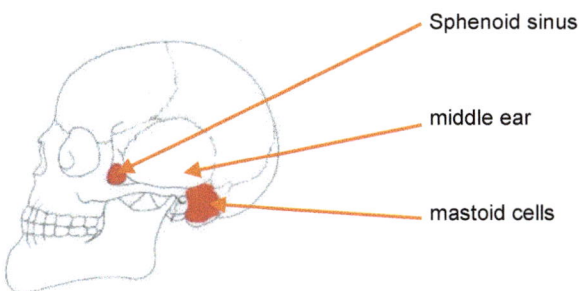

Sphenoid sinus

middle ear

mastoid cells

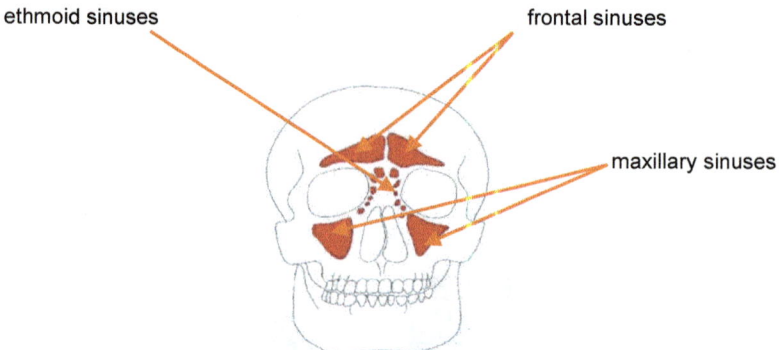

ethmoid sinuses   frontal sinuses

maxillary sinuses

There are also possible cavities under the dental seals, if your dentist had a bad day. All these cavities in our body must necessarily take part in the pressure equalization during diving. The mask interior is indeed outside of our body, but this space must also participate in pressure equalization.

Why pressure equalization?

Our body itself consists of about 2/3 of water and since water is almost incompressible we do not need to worry about it. More problematic are our cavities described above in the body, because these are filled with air and air can be compressed very well (squeeze). All our cavities in the body are lined with a so-called mucous membrane, which means nothing else than that the bones are covered by a more or less strongly perfused tissue.

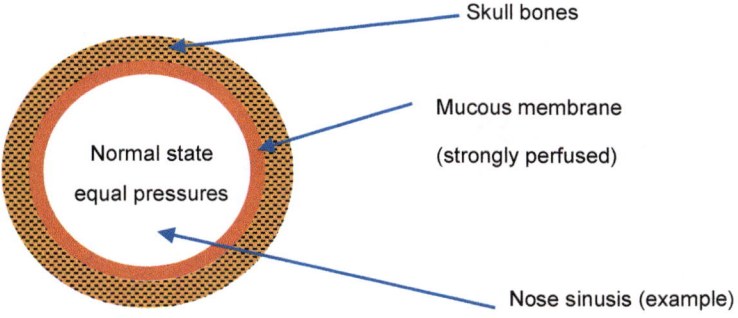

Skull bones

Mucous membrane

(strongly perfused)

Normal state

equal pressures

Nose sinusis (example)

The water pressure affecting us is also called "hydrostatic pressure". The hydrostatic pressure at the water surface is of course zero bar, because there is no water over us, which could put pressure on us. At the sea level, we are exposed only to the pressure exerted on us by the column of air above us (see outline "Atmospheric Pressure" on page 11), i.e. approximately one bar.

If we now dive without performing the pressure equalization, the surface pressure of one bar remains in our body and the external pressure, the hydrostatic pressure, increases. Thus, there is a pressure difference, which increases with increasing depth of water. As described under "inner blue coming " or "vacuum lung barotrauma / lung negative barotrauma", the relative negative pressure in our body sucks now tissue fluid into the mucous membranes, and increased by the concomitant reduction of the cavity, the pressure in it, i.e. adjusted to the ambient pressure.

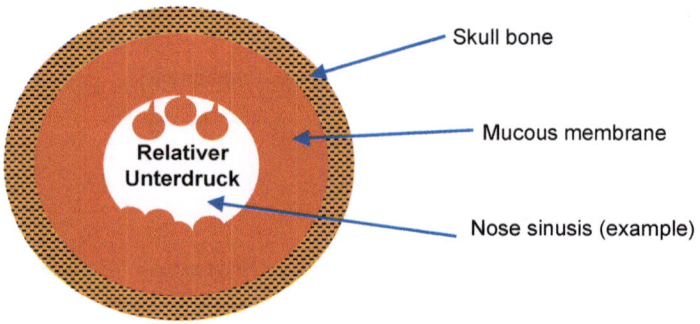

Skull bone

Mucous membrane

Nose sinusis (example)

Relativer Unterdruck

In the "ideal case" this happens until pressure equality prevails. However, this method of pressure adjustment is not recommended, as it is not only painful but also damages the body. Anyone who has ever attempted to dive with ABC gear while paying little attention to pressure adjustment will certainly confirm that the ears, specifically the eardrums and the surrounding tissue, hurt. Such an eardrum is quite elastic and does not crack so fast, but should that happen anyway, for the time being and maybe even forever, diving is over. But we will come to that later in chapter barotrauma (page 77).

1.5 The ear

Our ear is divided into three parts: the external ear, the middle ear and the inner ear (see outline).

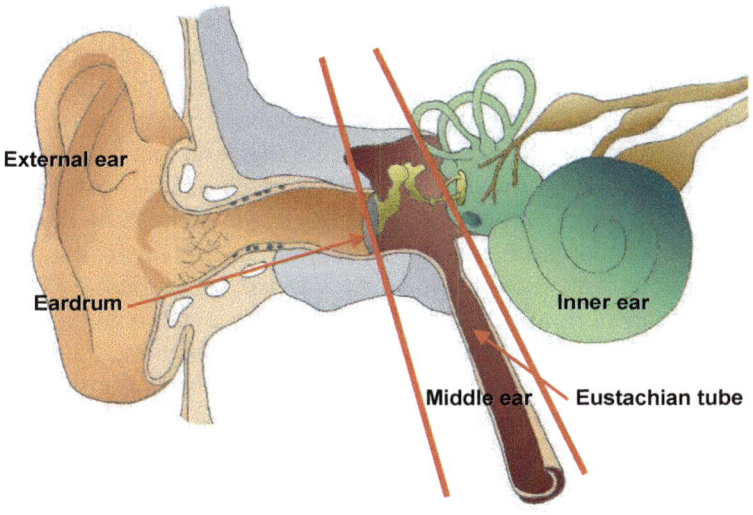

The main problem when diving is first and foremost our eardrum, because it is a wafer-thin sensitive membrane that reacts extremely well to pressure differences. The water penetrates into the outer auditory canal when diving and then rests directly on the eardrum. Increasing water pressure now pushes the eardrum towards the middle ear, stretching the eardrum. In order to prevent tearing, we must now make the pressure equalization, so in the middle ear build up the same pressure to bring the eardrum back to the normal position. There are different methods for this. The most widely used method is according to Valsalva. In doing so, the nose is closed by means of the thumb and forefinger, over the nose pocket of the mask, and then try to exhale through the nose (just like when cleaning the nose). Thereby we increase the pressure also within the cavities of our head and via the

Eustachian tube, also called the ear tube, the pressure propagates in the middle ear. If we now remove the fingers from the nose, the pressure is equal to the external pressure. When diving with the SCUBA, this generally works a bit easier than in freediving (diving with bated breath), but even without a SCUBA, great depths can be easily achieved. Practice makes perfect. If pressure equalization is successful, the eardrum is not stretched in one direction or the other. Of course, this process must be repeated with increasing water depth. Beginners can therefore keep their hands on the nose during rapid descents, since pressure equalization must be carried out continuously until the desired water depth is reached. This may seem complicated to the inexperienced, but be assured that after several dives, this pressure equalization becomes so normal that you almost unconsciously perform it. In any case, start immediately after leaving the water surface with the pressure equalization and do not wait until a pain sets in. Firstly, it can damage your ear drum and, secondly, it may cause your Eustachian tube to be compressed due to the negative pressure and then pressure equalization is no longer possible. If this happens, you must reduce your depth immediately, if necessary, to the water surface and then start the descent again. Keep in mind that your ear drum is a sensitive part of the body and take care of it. Also, make sure that a close-fitting wetsuit can close your ear to the outside, so there is a chance that the pressure inside your cranial cavities may be higher than the pressure in your external ear canal if the pressure balance is successful. To prevent damage to the ear drum, the hood of the dive suit must not be too tight; the ambient pressure must be able to act on both sides of the ear drum to prevent damage. However, to your relief, you are assured that you will not have to make pressure equalization when going up. The relative pressure decreases naturally by breathing, provided your eustachian tubes are open. In the case of a cold, the ear tube may be swollen and the pressure may be reduced slowly or, in the worst case, with great pain. So do not dive if you have a cold. And never mind to the idea to "protect" your ears with plugs. Just imagine what the rising ambient pressure will do with these plugs. In the first step, the plugs are pressed into your external auditory canal, which certainly will not happen without pain. Anyone who is pain resistant enough to ignore this is then ready for the second step. Once the plugs are firmly seated and cannot be pushed further, there is a relative negative pressure between the plug and the ear drum, because you have made the necessary pressure equalization during the descent. Now, the pressure inside your cranial cavity is greater than the pressure between the plug and the eardrum, and so we are back on the subject of "relative negative pressure"! In this case, your eardrum will overstretch outward and tear at worst. Conclusion:

No ear plugs when diving, if you love your ear drum.

In the interior of the mask, the same thing happens as in your body. The surface pressure is inside the mask interior at the time of descent, and because the mask body (silicone) is flexible, the mask is pressed more and more tightly against your face due to the increasing pressure. In order to avoid a relative negative pressure in the mask interior, simply breathe out some air through the nose. The mask will then lift off your face again. If you have exhaled too much air, which is completely harmless, the excessive air will simply escape at the edge of the mask. This process must be carried out again and again until reaching the maximum depth. If you do not balance the pressure difference this difference will damage your eyes. Because the relative negative pressure in the mask, similar to a cupping glass, drains body fluid into the tissue in the mask area. Because our eyes are mostly out of water, and the blood capillaries in the eye are just below the surface, they quickly take on damage, as can be seen from broken capillaries in the whites of the eye. If this happens to you, you should not dive until the capillaries are healed or an ophthalmologist gives you the okay to dive. Incidentally, the broken capillaries also like to hide under the eyelids (above and below). Take a closer look after the dive if you had trouble ventilating the mask interior.

1.6 The regulator – Breathing under water

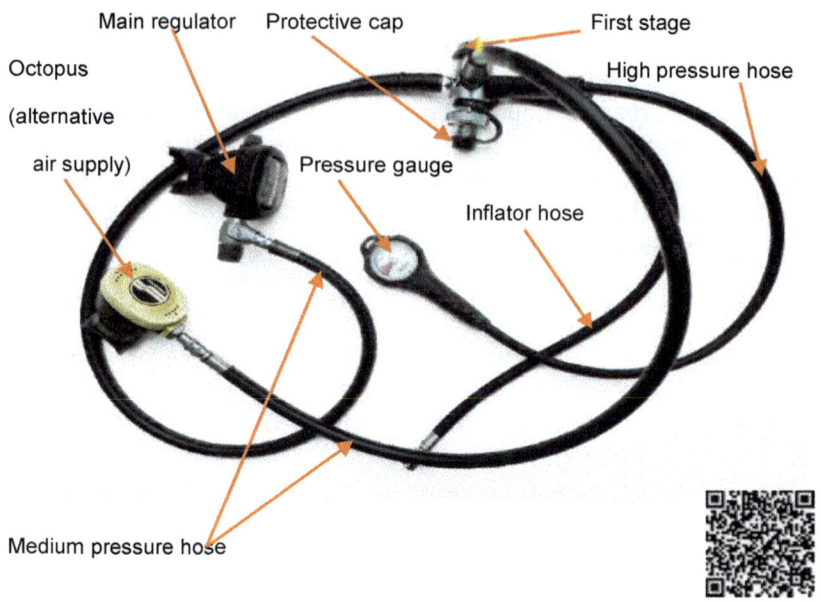

Main regulator   Protective cap   First stage

Octopus   High pressure hose

(alternative

air supply)   Pressure gauge

Inflator hose

Medium pressure hose

In short: We do not describe the assembly of all the equipment here, as this is the task of the dive guide, instructor assistant or instructor. But if you still want to be prepared, take a look at this short video (see the QR code above).

The regulator, of course, does not regulate your breath. You can still breathe as often and as deeply as you like. However, the regulator regulates the pressure of your breathing air. We have already learned that pressure increases with increasing water depth. However, our lung musculature is able to handle a pressure difference in the millibar range (1 bar equals 1000 millibar). In practice this means that you will no longer be able to breathe in at a depth of one to two meters without the regulator. So, the regulator ensures that the air you need is always at the same pressure as in your environment. Thus, your lungs have the same pressure as outside your body and you can breathe just as easily as on the surface.

Note: Damage (barotrauma) and problems arise only when there is a pressure difference. See page 77.

A modern regulator consists of three parts. The first stage, which is screwed by hand wheel to the valve of the tank, converts the tank pressure of 200 or 300 bar into an ambient pressure-dependent medium pressure. The second stage, which uses a system of pistons and diaphragms to set the pressure of the first stage exactly to the ambient pressure and the medium pressure hose, which connects both stages. At the second stage, which is technically the regulator, is the mouthpiece mounted, which keeps your mouth watertight by biting the bite warts and enclosing the lip of the mouthpiece with your lips. Take care not to bite too hard, because the biting warts are also made of silicone and can be bitten off. In addition, a too-tight bite is detrimental to a relaxed dive. If you now put the regulator in your mouth, the first breath should always be the exhalation. If you get used to exhale first, you will have less breathing problems under water, in case of share air, or you took the second stage out of your mouth. Take a deep breath first, take the second stage in your mouth and blow strongly into the second stage. First, you will notice that the exhalation membrane is not sticking and working properly, and second, carry any water, sand or salt out of the second stage. Of course, there shouldn't be such foreign particles in a well-kept regulator, but for sure it is safe. Well, after you have blown off vigorously, it's time for the first inhalation. Do the same with the second second stage, also called octopus. The octopus, which name is probably given because of the number of hoses that come from the first stage, is an alternate air supply that you can give to your partner as needed to prevent the share air. The air you breathe in is cleaned and dried to a high standard and is absolutely clean when the dive center or base operator has fulfilled his duty to maintain his breathing air compressor, which can be expected generally. That's why the instructor on site must breathe this air too. If the air does not "taste", you can tell the base leader or the instructor in a friendly way. It can always happen that a filter of the compressor has exceeded its lifetime during the filling process and the air then develops its own "taste". A responsible base manager will then immediately give you another tank and inspect the compressor. In addition to the two second stages, we also find here the medium pressure hose for the Buoyancy Device (BCD) and the pressure gauge, which shows us the current air pressure in the tank.

Well, after you are ready to make your first breath underwater, we come to the specific things that you need to keep in mind. **It is very important that you keep in mind that the breathing air given by the regulator is always exactly under the pressure prevailing in your environment <u>at that moment</u>.** For example, if you are sitting in the pool at a depth of 2 meters, you have a pressure of 1.2 bar in your lungs. That is quite wanted and absolutely okay. **As long as you stay in this depth**. The trick with the lung-automatic adaptation to the ambient pressure is that the regulator delivers the inhaled air in compressed form and thus makes breathing possible. For example, if you have inhaled deeply at the water surface and there are now 5 liters of air under the pressure of 1 bar in your lungs, you have 20% more air in your lungs at the same depth of inhalation at a depth of 2 meters, as the pressure now is 1.2 bar. So 6 liters of air. In both cases, your lungs are filled and more does not fit into it. However, they have in comparison to the surface thus 1 liter of breathing air more in the lungs. That doesn't matter at all as long as you stay there or dive deeper. But if you want to go up because you get bored or you want to look after the children, you have to remember that you have to exhale this liter of air which is too much in your lungs. So get accustomed always to exhale during the going up phase, <u>in such a case</u>. It's better to arrive at the water surface with an empty lung than with a ruptured lung. Because that's exactly what can happen if you do not exhale enough while diving with the SCUBA. For sure you cannot exhale the entire time, for example, if you ascend from 20 meters, that's not necessary of course. **Time plays a big role here.** For example, if you get up quickly during your pool dive so that you can look out of the water and do not exhale the compressed air that you have inhaled at the bottom of the pool, your lungs become overstretched and can even rupture in the worst case. Because this liter of air, which you have "too much" in your lungs, has to be exhaled, because only 5 liters fit into your lungs. The volume of your lungs will not change, but the pressure in it depends on the ambient pressure and is above the pool once 1 bar and at the bottom of the pool 1.2 bar. So the air has to come out during going up and since getting up is fast, the air has to go out fast too. Or you can breathe normally and take a lot of time going up. As a result, you breathe the air always under the ambient pressure and thus the pressure slowly but surely reduces and nothing can happen to your lungs. As part of a normal dive, which leads you to 20 meters, you do not have to pay special attention to anything. Go slowly and comfortably down and up again, the regulator will always give you the breathing air under ambient pressure and as long as you continue to breathe and don't stop breathing when going up, nothing can happen. However, if, for whatever reason, you feel that you have to go up as quickly as possible, you must take care to exhale the surplus air. It is best to omit such emergency emerge, these are dangerous and really tolerable only in great need. If you feel the urge to breathe in during an inevitable emergency ascent from greater depths, be sure to stay at the current depth and never breathe while "shooting" up! By inhaling, you prevent the exhalation of the expanding breathing gas and risk a lung rupture. However, if it is unavoidable and you need to inhale, because you feel the irresistible urge, then you inhale only briefly and shallowly and exhale deep and long. Again, it should be mentioned again that such an emergency ascent occurs extremely rare. I did this for training purposes only and have not done it for years because it can harm my health. If you follow the instructions of your instructor, who is always at your side, nothing can happen to you.

If, after the dive, you rinse your equipment in fresh water, be sure not to push the air knob on the two second stages. If you do this while the stages are in the fresh water, water will penetrate into the medium pressure hose and from there into the first stage, damaging it. The same applies to the opening in the first stage, through which our breathing gas gets into the first stage. This would also cause water to enter the first stage and damage it. Covering this opening with a dust and thread protection cap is NOT sufficient; keep the opening firmly closed with your thumb during the flushing process. The professionals flush their regulator when connected and under pressure. So no water can penetrate into the regulator. However, this procedure is rather uncommon on dive centers and can also lead to injuries because the entire device is heavy and unwieldy. On the bases there is usually a water-filled sink available, in which you should only flush your regulator if this pool is not used for the entire equipment of all divers. If someone, for example, have rinsed his foot lets in this water and you are now flushing your regulator in the same water, it could not only lead to unusual taste sensations on the mouthpiece of your regulator, but also lead to a possible contamination of your regulator. Rinse your regulator better under running water or in a basin, which is reserved only for regulators.

1.7 Lifejacket / Stabilizing Jacket / BCD – Buoyancy device

Adjustment straps   Filling hose (pleated tube)   Overpressure valve

Medium

pressure -

hose

Inflator -

connection

Zip pockets

D-rings (for

fixing

material)

Waist belt

weight

pockets

with

quick release

Regulator- and/or hose holder

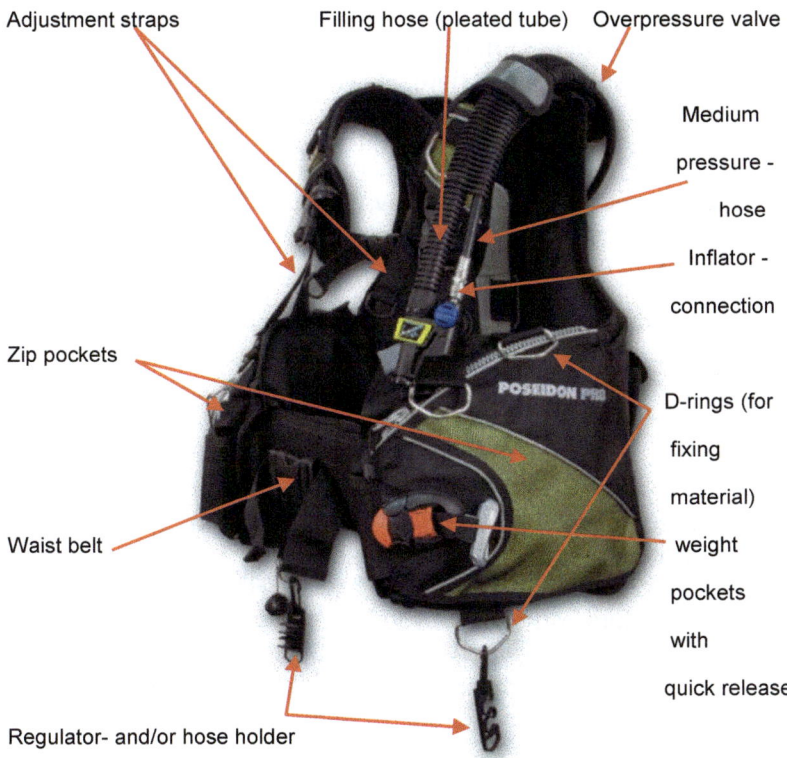

The main task of a rescue and BCD (Buoyancy Device) is already adequately described with their naming, but modern specimens can do even more. So have these "Jackets", as they are colloquially called worn, not only bags for the weights and for carried objects such as lamps, buoys or safety ropes (reels), but they also include the mounting options (backplate and straps) for the tank. Some jackets are even designed to carry double tanks. In addition, there are jackets, so-called "wings", where the buoyancy bladders are left and right of the tank(s), which allows a more comfortable position while diving. Tec divers (technical divers) like them, due to various advantages (larger volume) to a "normal" jacket, especially. What they all have in common is the fact that, as a rule, they do not meet the demand for a faint-proof situation on the water surface. The variety of jackets is very large, so we cannot go into detail here. However, this applies to all parts of the diving equipment, and since this book is not a catalog, but a textbook, we renounce to present all possible variations.

If you would like to know what is available and what it should be used for, we urge you to visit the instructor or the dive shop of your choice.

The rescue aspect of a jacket is lying in the fact that we can fill it via a medium- or low-pressure hose (inflator) or even with our exhaled air and thus, following the Archimedean principle, use it as a buoyancy. Please **absolutely** pay attention to the following: If you inflate your jacket underwater with the inflator, be very careful and only put very short blasts of air into the jacket. The lower the water depth you are in, the shorter the air blast you put into the jacket. For example, pushing the inflator for one second at 3 meters can mean an unwanted ascent. However, the same time at 30 meters can be clearly too short. Practice the handling of the inflator thoroughly and in different water depths. And should you have "pushed" too much air into the jacket and "shoot up", remember that you need to exhale when you love your health. However, there are other ways to stop this unwanted ascent. So you can use the pleated tube (filling hose) or the drain button on the opposite side of the pleated tube connection, in the shoulder area, at any time very effectively to deflate the air from your jacket. For many jackets it is sufficient to grab the entire pleated tube and pull it to release air. Be sure to familiarize yourself with your equipment before diving with it. The "floating" underwater, also called buoyancy or hydrostatic balance, is the biggest hurdle for beginners and you will need some dives until you are satisfied with your buoyancy. But that's okay, practice makes the master (German saying).

Practice adjusting buoyancy at shallow water (up to 5 meters) and make sure nothing is above you (boat, bridge, surfers, swimmers ...) and furthermore make sure to exhale deeply when going up unintentional and too fast. Probably this will happen, but regarding my advice you will be prepared. Keep in mind that your lungs are also something like a buoyant body, and as you inhale, following Archimedes' principles, you increase your volume and have the same effect as filling your jacket. Of course, the same applies to the exhalation, because if you notice that it goes up unintentionally, it can be enough to exhale deeply to slow or stop the ascent. That's what we divers call "fine-tuning" through breathing. You will find out, after some practice, that adjusting buoyancy is not as difficult as it sounds. Even after a few dives adjusting buoyancy becomes a matter of course for you and it happens almost casually and without thinking. Why we have to adjust buoyancy at all, i.e. constantly have to control our up and down, will be explained in the following section.

1.8 The SCUBA / the tank / compressed air cylinder

In everyday use, the compressed air cylinder / tank or SCUBA is optionally referred to as a tank, tank, or even compressed air cylinder. Mostly called tank. Whatever the tank is called, what is meant is always a compressed air tank which, as a rule, is under a pressure of approx. 200 - 220 bar after filling process. As a diving beginner it is sufficient to know that the tank is made of steel or aluminum and the valve is usually made of bronze or brass. If possible, a tank is stored lying in daily use, so that it cannot tip over. First, it hurts very much when the tank falls on your foot and, secondly, there is a real danger that the tank will fall so badly that the valve will be damaged and the compressed air will flow out as a result of the high pressure. In such a case, the tank, if it has room enough to take off, set off under an extremely loud and hearing-impairing noise and cause massive damage. So be careful when dealing with the tank. If you want to connect the regulator, remove the dust and thread cap that is in the valve and check the connection thread for cleanliness and damage. Then hand-tighten the first stage of the regulator or let your instructor do it.

Removing the dust cap

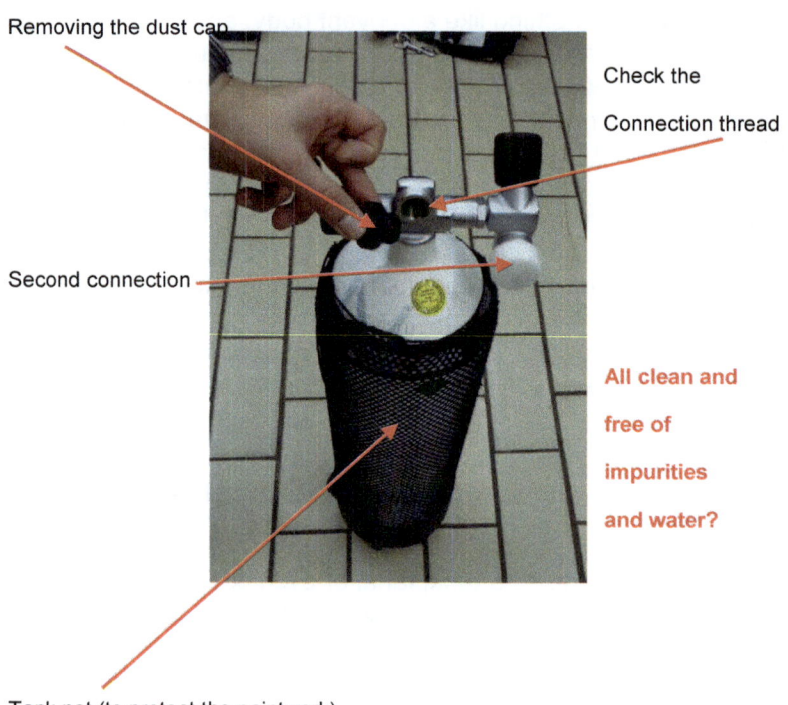

Check the

Connection thread

Second connection

All clean and

free of

impurities

and water?

Tank net (to protect the paintwork)

Optical inspection of the first stage!

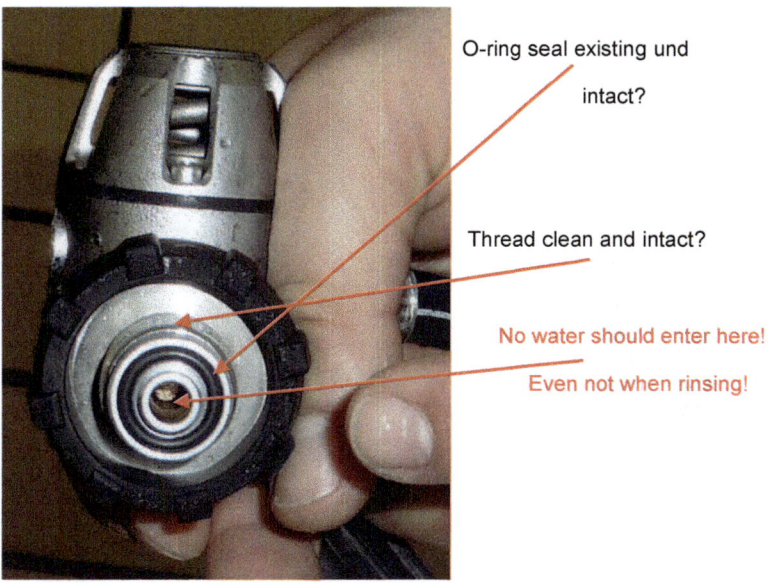

O-ring seal existing und intact?

Thread clean and intact?

No water should enter here!
Even not when rinsing!

1.9 The wetsuit

Water is a good conductor of heat, and we know that from our childhood, when we were, after a very short time, "pulled" out of the water by our mother, because our lips had already turned blue as a result of hypothermia. What we have ignored in our childhood can be a problem when diving. A freezing diver is unfocused and hypothermia leads to health damage. A freezing diver is a bad diver. Water conducts heat about 25 times as much as the air. That would mean, at least theoretically, that we will cool down 25 times as fast as in the air. However, the body has regulatory mechanisms that can prevent this, to a certain point. But even very good diving suits cannot avoid the cooling, they can only slow the cooling process down.

Wetsuit, one-piece

Overall with attached hood

Separate hood

Three finger glove 6,5 mm

Five finger glove 3,2 mm

Foot let / boot

34

In addition to the various wetsuit types, there is of course also the cold protection for hands and feet, also made of neoprene. We choose our diving suit according to the requirement and size of the purse. The standard diving suit is the so-called wetsuit, which is called so because the water penetrates between the body and suit, warmed up there and, depending on the design of the suit, little or no exchange. The less exchange, the more we take a bath in our self heated water. These suits are relatively inexpensive and just right for the beginner. Therefore, we will only deal with this suit closer and simply name the other options. There are, as almost always, no limits upwards. Neither at the desired heat insulation nor at the price. In the order of thermal insulation follows next the semi-dry suit, which, by design, keeps the warm water better than the wetsuit. Then follows the membrane or tri laminate suit, which does not allow any water to the body, except the hands, when no dry-diving gloves are used, and the face. In the same category, namely the dry suits, belongs the neoprene dry suit, which keeps the body not only dry, but also very warm, because it has a high thermal insulation capacity. All these suits isolate our body more or less well against the cold of the water, but also have the added effect of protection against injury. Some extreme environmentalists among divers demand the prohibition of wearing gloves or diving suits with long arms and legs, so as not to seduce the diver to touch reefs or animals underwater. They believe that only this measure will enable environmentally friendly diving. I have already experienced dive center leaders in Egypt who forbid wearing gloves during the dive. I react to that with a clear "yes/no"! In the military this is called "learning through pain" and I reject this educational lesson as a responsible citizen. Of course, we should not touch anything underwater and also not touch anything by accident, that is clear and needs no further mention, but what if we make a buoyancy error or completely unintentionally rub a reef with our knee? What if we have to use the hand to prevent breaking a coral? This list of eventualities could go on for a long time, but the principle is always the same. No matter how much we try to stay as far away as possible from the objects of our diver's desire, contact with them is sometimes unavoidable. Injuries, such as cuts or abrasions that we can get ourselves under water, heal abroad, with a lot of water contact, heat and often low hygiene, only very bad and can spoil the whole holiday. So don't touch anything underwater, „float" like a professional and make sure not to touch anything at all and wear a diving suit which protect you for minor injuries.

Our wetsuit is made of neoprene, a foamed rubber compound introduced by the company DuPont in 1938 under the name "Neoprene", which is very easy to process and glue and also has a very good insulation property. As a rule, our "Wet suit" consists of a pair of trousers, also known as Long John, and a jacket with attached hood. One-piece wet suits (see above) are often used. Zippers facilitate entry, but also form a cold bridge, where water can enter and exit. Neoprene is, as already mentioned above, a foamed material which has millions of bubbles inside, similar to a sponge. In contrast to the sponge these bubbles in the neoprene are not connected but isolated from each other. This means that the suit will not be able to soak, and the water will bead off it. To increase the durability of the material neoprene, the suits are laminated, so provided with a fabric layer. Although this also reduces the extensibility of the neoprene, but the longer durability justifies this measure.

Of course, the wet suit has not only advantages, that would be too nice. Its biggest disadvantage is its biggest advantage, because the high insulating capacity of the material is based on the trapped gas bubbles in the neoprene and gases are compressible. This means that the suit is compressed with increasing depth of water and thus also increasing pressure, and thus not only loses insulation, but also volume; he just gets thinner. Thus, our wetsuit and everything that is made of neoprene on our body loses its volume during descent and thus, according to Archimedes, buoyancy. Attention: During ascent this volume comes back. So that we do not stand on 20 meters water depth as nailed down on the seabed, which we should avoid for environmental and animal welfare reasons anyway, so we have to regain buoyancy somehow.

And here comes the aspect of taring into the game. We just put some air via the inflator in our jacket and get back the volume, which our neoprene has lost in the descent phase. And already, after a little practice, we float again above the things, so the bottom of the sea. A question from Archimedes.

I have mentioned the name "Archimedes" a few times and now it is time to explain it.

Archimedes was an important mathematician and physicist of the antique (about 287 - 212 BC). His most important theorem for us divers is, freely translated:

A body that is completely or partially submerged in a liquid experiences as much buoyancy how the amount of fluid displaced by it weighs.

We let this sentence "melt on the tongue" (just another German saying)! It contains important things. It states that the buoyancy the body experiences, so we divers including our equipment, depends on the amount of fluid displaced and on the type of fluid displaced.

So if we weigh 100 kg (mass) with a diving volume of 110 liter and then jump into the water, we will not go down. So we displace 110 liters of salt water, for example, in the Mediterranean and that means 110 x 1.03 kilograms per liter, i.e. 113.3 kilograms of lift compared to 100 kg downforce. We swim at the water surface, as we experience an effective buoyancy of 13.3 kilograms, On the one hand, that is great, because we can relax, but on the other hand, we do not want to stay on the surface, we like to dive. So we have to eliminate this buoyancy and even steer it.

1.10 The weights

For this we have to carry weights with us, which compensate this buoyancy, and there has proven the use of lead (11.3 kg / dm³). Heavy and cheap. Of course you could also take gold (19.3 kg /

dm³), that's even more massive, but not cheap. Always try to carry as little lead as possible, but as much as you need. The weight, which makes the descent easier or possible, is also a burden and requires strength and endurance when swimming. In addition to the traditional lead belt you now have the opportunity to carry your weights in special pockets of your BCD.

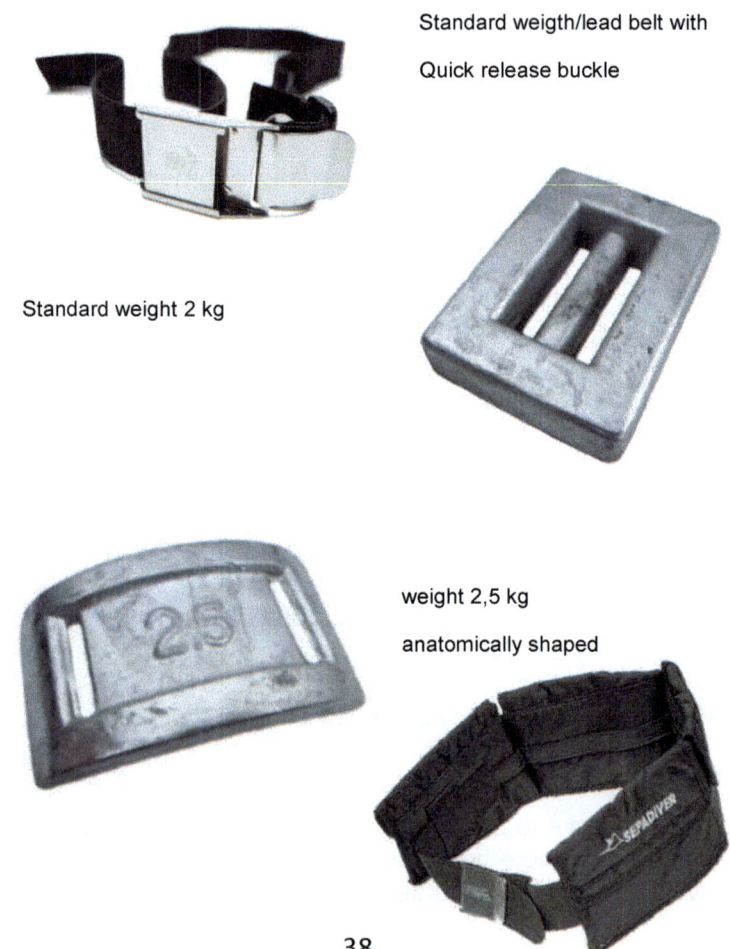

Standard weigth/lead belt with

Quick release buckle

Standard weight 2 kg

weight 2,5 kg

anatomically shaped

Soft weight belt with pockets

Soft weight. Little lead pearls which are more comfortable to wear as a stiff lead weight.

The soft lead snuggles up the body contours and does not press punctually.

The correct amount of weight can be determined relatively easily, but is sometimes also a matter of personal preference. Equip yourself completely and go into the water in which you want to dive. Empty your BCD and fill your lungs with a deep breath and then lie down on the water surface. If you go down now, you have packed too much lead, because now you should swim. So reduce the weight/lead. If that works with swimming, then exhale deeply. Now you should go down. However, this rough method of finding the right amount of lead only applies to this configuration of equipment and this type of water. If you go from salt to fresh water or change your suit, you must repeat this test. In the IDA Logbook you will find a column where you can make a note of the respective lead quantities so that you do not have to repeat these tests each time.

However, if you have to emerge quickly, regardless of any losses, then you simply drop the lead. Each lead belt and each bag in the jacket, has a quick release device. But be aware before that you cannot slow down this fast ascent and will go up unstoppably to the water surface. So exhale during the ascent to get rid of the continuously expanding air in your lungs. The release of the weight belt is really the last possibility to prevent an accident. And

39

make sure that nothing is above you. So, always look up when going up.

1.11 Sign Language

Many people dive to escape the noise and bustle above water for a few minutes or even hours and to enjoy the tranquility. This is also an essential aspect why diving has many friends. Even the largest "talkative character" must necessarily shut up under water so as not to drown. But sometimes you have to tell your partner something important, for example, if your own breathing gas supply is running low, probably because you forgot to take a look at the pressure gauge. It rarely happens but it can happen when underwater is so exciting or the camera does not do what it should do. For basic communication, there are the underwater hand signs. They should always be simple, clear and above all else common around the world. How good is the most beautiful self-invented hand sign, if only my dive partner and I know what is meant? Therefore, we show you here only the most important and international hand signs, which should nevertheless be practiced before each dive with the respective partner. Hand signals are clear to give!

The static hand signs, such as Okay or ascent or descent are shown in the following only as a picture, the dynamic hand signals we have inserted as a short film, by QR code. The critical reader may note that a hand signal that says "out of air" or "I have problems with pressure balance" should not make much sense over water. This is correct and well aware of the author of these lines. These underwater hand signals were recorded solely over water to make them clearly visible.

Question Okay? Answer Okay! (Given from near)

Question Okay? Answer Okay! Given from middle distance.

Question Okay? Answer Okay! Given from great distance.

Go down / going down / descent!

42

Go up / going up / ascent!

How is the pressure on your pressure gauge? How many air do you still have?

100 bar residual pressure!

Residual pressure reached! 50 bar residual pressure!

Out of air situation / No air anymore! Immediate request to give air!

Something is wrong! Repeated turning of the hand in the wrist.

Problems with the pressure equalization / pressure balance!

Emergency over or under water! Clear up and down movement of the arms!

One-sided!

Emergency over or under water! Clear up and down movement of the arms!

Both-sides!

49

1.12 Tips for your Discover Scuba dive!

Please consider, before, during and after your introductory dive, that your Instructor, Instructor Assistant, Group Leader or Guide is much more knowledgeable about scuba diving than you are. Of course you do not have to put your common sense in the locker room, but if you get instructions from the dive staff, stick to it. The staff is responsible for you as long as you are in their hands and the colleagues have a great interest in not only surviving, but also enjoying the introductory dive. If you dive, do not go further than 2 to 3 meters away from your guide, depending on the visibility underwater, it may already be too far and remember that he guides you, not the other way round. He knows the sights and possibly dangers on the dive site better than you. Do not touch anything under water, you could injure yourself or damage the flora and fauna. Keep in mind that there are still many divers after you who want to see the same as you. After the dive, it is best to leave the equipment care to the base staff or, if you want to do it yourself, ask the staff how to do it. There is something to consider, especially with the regulator.

The Introductory dive chapter is now over, and now you know, when you have read and understood everything, what is necessary to enjoy a nice and relaxed introductory dive under the guidance of your Instructor. If, after this dive, you realize that this is going to be your sport and you want to experience the underwater world even more intensively, you should, as it is prescribed in many countries, attend a complete diving course. Which way you go there, is up to you. The offer of the various diving organisations is great. However, I am here allowed to promote my association, the IDA (International Diving Association), because there I am a well educated instructor and happy with the IDA for more than 20 years and can recommend the diving instructors, instructor assistants and dive guides.

2. Additional equipment

Now that we've studied the basic things necessary to do a Introductory dive and that every trained diver should know by heart, let's turn to the things and issues that are just as important, but makes the difference between a well trained scuba diver and a diver in training. In addition, we now deepen some statements about the equipment

2.1 The divers knife – a tool, no weapon -

As you can easily see above, there are many different diving knives, in all sizes, shapes and colors. Depending on the design, they can be worn on the leg, fastened to the jacket or even screwed onto the medium-pressure hose. A diving knife is first and foremost a tool that we need to cut ourselves or our partner off a leash, fishing line or fishing net if necessary. The blade should be stable and form a unit together with the handle that does not give way at every stress. For most knives, however, you will not be able to test this requirement because the plastic handle cannot be removed. With the exception of knives made of titanium, all scuba knives are susceptible to rust, so you should always lightly grease your knife with petroleum jelly and check the protective layer from time to time. But even if you do not do that, your diving knife will last a long time. Like all other equipment, the knife has to be rinsed with fresh water after the dive and dried in the shade. Some divers believe that the blade of the knife should not be sharpened to avoid injury. Okay, the idea is not outlandish, but anyone who has actually landed in a fishing net and got tangled up in it, will agree that the blade of the knife cannot be sharp enough. So much confidence must we have in our abilities that we can handle knives with care. In the local kitchen that works very well too. A diving knife is an important part of diving equipment and not a toy. Those who are afraid of knives (xyrophobia, aichmophobia or optionally also machairophobia) can also do very well with suitable scissors or use the cutter shown below. However, both tools have the disadvantage to be useless when cutting thick ropes and who has ever tried to remove a rope from the propeller and the drive shaft, will plead for the knife.

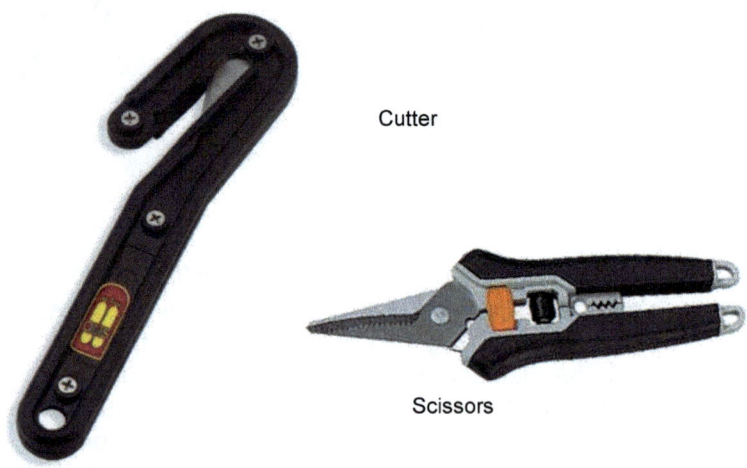

Cutter

Scissors

Scissors and knife combined

2.2 Diver's watch

The diver's watch is more of a statement today than a much used tool underwater. With the diver's watch today one shows rather its affiliation to the group of the divers, than that one uses them really for diving. This is not because the watches are superfluous, but it is the advancement of technology in general, and in particular, the invention of the dive computer. A good dive computer you get today for less than 400.- Euro. And this computer does all the calculation for you. Since you cannot think and combine well, depending on the depth, anyway, the dive computer is a great help for many.

Adjustable rotating ring

Easy to read luminescent

clock-face

Scratch- and pressure

resistant glass (Mineral or

better sapphire)

clock luminescent

Pressure resistant and

stainless

metal housing

(at least 200 m waterproof)

O-ring sealed crown

Adjustable watch strap

In the past, the diver's watch was an important instrument for determining decompression times, and if the computer ever fails, which is very rare but not impossible, you can safely end a dive today by using the clock and decompression table. In addition, a beautiful diver's watch is also a gem and you know what you could wish for Christmas or your birthday. Only return your diver's watch to authorized specialist workshops for repair and battery replacement. After every service, the water resistance of the watch must be checked and not all watch shops can do that.

If you want to buy a diver's watch, pay attention to the following details:

Buy the watch from a stockist.

The glass should be made of sapphire crystal, as this is particularly scratch-resistant.

The crown should be screwed and O-ring sealed.

The rotary ring may rotate counterclockwise only to prevent accidental twisting of the rotary ring. Otherwise the dive time seems too short and a decompression accident may be possible.

The clock should be tested at least to a depth of 200 meters. Not because you dive so deep but because that is a quality feature for the tightness of the clock.

The bracelet should be long enough to wear the watch over the diving suit.

The figures and the clocks/pointers should be luminescent to guarantee a good readability even at Night dives.

2.3 The depth gauge

The best diver's watch is nothing worth if we don't know how deep we have been. The trio, watch, depth gauge and decompression table has been the tool of choice for decades to make a correct decompression. Generally the depth gauge doesn't measure the depth but the ambient pressure. These measured pressure will be transmit via levers and gears on a shaft to which the pointer is attached. The first depth gauges worked after the system Boyle-Mariotte and were made of a pipe which was open only at one side. These pipe was fixed above a scale, which showed the depth in meter. Depending on the pressure, the water penetrated into the pipe and at the separation surface water / air you could read the depth. Simple and inexpensive, but outdated and inaccurate.

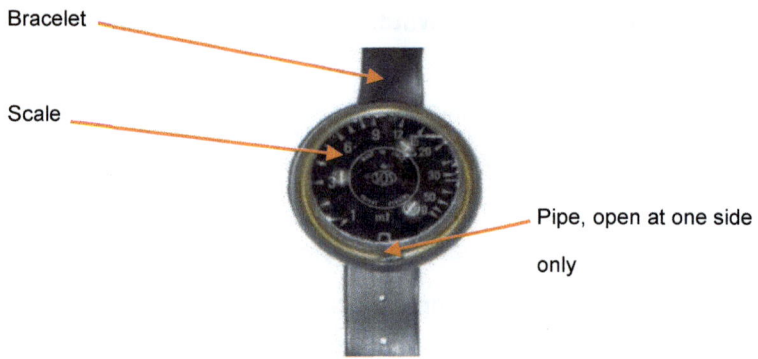

Bracelet

Scale

Pipe, open at one side only

Today's standard depth gauges work with a membrane that absorbs the pressure and passes it via the lever and gearwheels to the pointer.

Today's standard depth gauges

Half- and quarter gearweels with lever

Clock/pointer

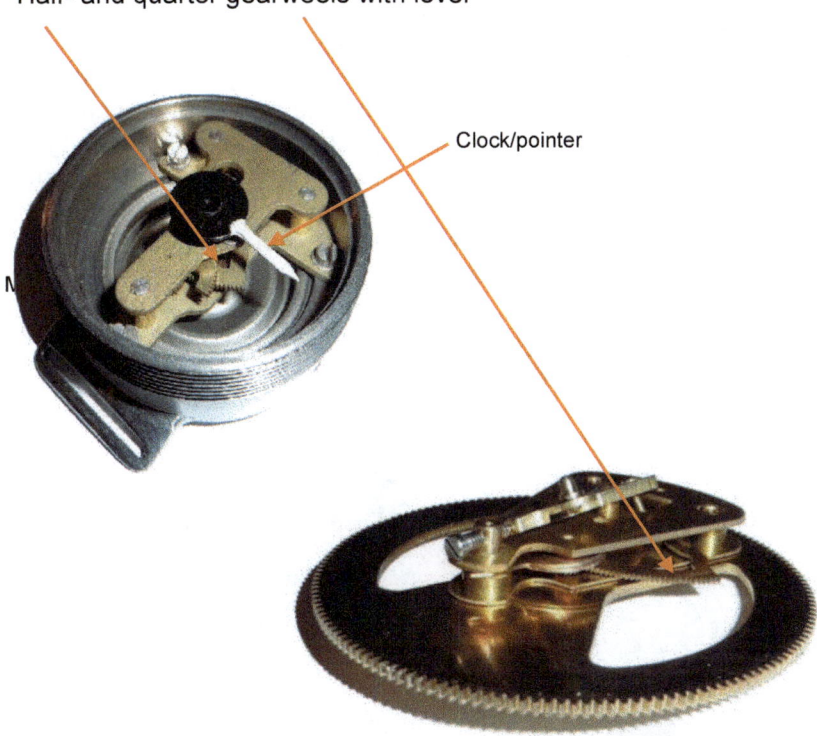

Apart from that, the same criteria apply to the depth gauge as for the diver's watch, because in the end it is also a watch, which however shows the water depth. Another difference is that you have not to replace a battery because it hasn't one. However, since there were resourceful people who have united the clock, the depth gauge and also the decompression table in one device, the depth gauge has become quite obsolete today. If you still want to buy one, pay attention to the following details. The dial should be luminescent (fluorescent), so that it can read well even at night dives, without having to light it up any longer. The decompression levels, 3 to 12 meters, should be highlighted to make it easier to stop at these steps. The glass of the depth gauge should be made of sapphire crystal, as this is particularly scratch-resistant and a height adjustment and zero point adjustment would be nice to have. These two features have only the higher quality depth gauge integrated. They serve to adapt to the different ambient pressures at the sea and on the mountain lake as well as the temperature adjustment. Some depth gauges also have a so-called drag pointer, which stops at the maximum depth of the dive and is therefore a great help when there's a need to a decompression. The bracelet should be long enough to be worn even over a drysuit.

2.4 The divers computer

Again, who would have guessed, many different models, which often have got so many features that one of us is hopelessly overwhelmed. As with every computer. Such a computer is a very practical and recommended tool. These devices can do much more than just show dive time and depth. And if you have informed yourself on the Internet or at a trade fair about their abilities, you finally come to the conclusion that these things often can do much more than you need. But that does not matter, because you are not forced to retrieve all skills and it comes in handy your computer is also your logbook That's not so bad. So you can't forget to log your dives. The Cosmiq from the company deepblu not only offers you a logbook function mobile app on a website, but also combines them with a "facebook" for divers. The fact that some computers also display the pressure of your tank in digital form by means of transmitters at the first stage, is chic, too, although you should rather still have a look on the pressure gauge. Because even a battery in the computer can quit its duty and the law of Murphy has taught us that something usually happens in a not suitable moment. Because a dive computer calculates your own decompression time and depth based on dive time, depth, and dive profile, you cannot pass the computer on to a buddy or your spouse if you no longer want to dive. Of course, the computer does not know that the user has changed now and then your wife may have to decompress for a very long time, even though it's only her first dive. You would then have more time for serious dive stories at the bar but if your wife has decompressed to the end, there could be trouble. So, dive computers cannot be easily lent to other divers. Before buying a dive computer, consult a stockist and inform yourself at like-minded people. Also, keep in mind that your eyes are not as fit as they used to be in youth and there may be problems reading the often small digits and letters. I am 58 and I have problems with the little digits. My colleague used a specially-made magnifying glass for this purpose, but that's not for everyone and perhaps a little bit ridiculous. Care and treatment see watch and depth gauge. **Tip**: If you have the opportunity to rinse your equipment in rainwater and thus in nearly lime-free water, you should do so.

Because next to the sand is the lime from our tap water, a mineral that can adversely affect the function of our equipment.

2.5 The divers flag

Divers "show their flag" and should do so in the water to protect themselves. In the international flag alphabet, there is the "A" flag or "Alpha" better known among divers as Alpha Flag.

2 Meter

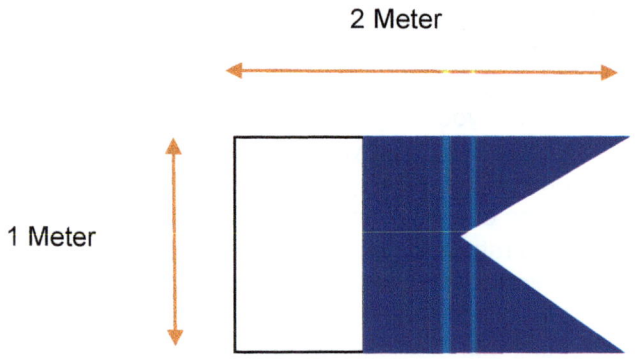

1 Meter

In most European countries this flag is set when divers are underwater. It is usually hoisted by the captain and has, according to the international rules, also a minimum size that we diver in everyday life can't comply. But even the smallest flag is better than none. Because how should skipper or surfers know about the divers below them? In choppy seas, the bubbles of the exhaled air are barely visible and the skipper on the bridge at 20 meters does not see anything which is smaller than a seagull anyway.

The alpha flag shown below is often set by divers or pulled along on a leash. Whether this flag in case of doubt is lawful, the first court ruling must still clarify. But even this flag is better than none. However, there is still the maritime road system, which determines where in the sea may be dived at all.

In the harbour area, which is marked in the respective nautical chart, diving is generally prohibited. But remind the possibility to get a permission if there's a urgent need to dive there.

If in doubt, ask the water police or the harbor master. Otherwise you bring yourself or your bank account balance in danger.

Even if your dive mates, for their convenience, are lazy and do not use a Alpha , stay firm and set the flag on the jetty near which you must remain, on the dive boat or on the beach. Of course, it makes no sense to set an Alpha flag and then dive at a great distance. But I have nowhere found an exact distance, there are only instructions to the skipper to pass with a large distance and with little speed. Of course you can also carry the flag with you on a small rope. Be careful, however, that you can quickly release the rope if it gets tangled somewhere or lands in the rotating shaft of a boat. Otherwise, it could be that the rotating shaft unwinds its rope and you immediately with. Then it goes "round" and your health will, in all likelihood, suffer, I prefer the fixed attachment of the flag, usually with a basic weight of 2 to 4 kg and then remain within 10 meters of the flag. If I want to go somewhere else, I'll take the flag to another place. If the small flag is too insecure for you and you are skilled in craftsmanship, just build your own alpha flag, including a buoy. Styrofoam buoys are available in specialized shops for fishing or on the internet, a large alpha flag in the dive shop, in the boat accessories shop or on the Internet and the aluminum tube in every hardware store. As a counterweight, so that the flag does not tip over, a simple weight from your weight belt has been proven. For your own safety never dive "without". The flag shown below, the so-called American Michigan flag, is also used in many countries as a dive flag, but is not an official flag signal.

61

It is widely used in Canada and the US, but even the US Navy is committed to the Alpha Flag. In Europe, the alpha flag is and remains the matter of choice!

2.6 The compass

Surely you have ever wondered how the divers orientate themselves underwater in case of poor visibility. Holistic, very simple. Okay, it's not quite as easy as I put it here, but most divers who are in "their" area know every stone and every fish by their first name and thus have a huge advantage. If you have often frequented your favorite dive site and you no longer need to focus on the handling of your scuba equipment and buoyancy, you'll find there are plenty of landmarks underwater to help you to find your way. In a course called Underwater Orientation or Compass Diving, you will learn all the skills you need to find your way underwater. A very important tool is, just like on land, the compass. There are several ways to wear it and you can choose how you like it best. As a console, including clock and depth gauge, on the arm by means of a bracelet or in a console on the high-pressure hose of the pressure gauge. Even with a retractor, a self-winding stainless steel rope, the compass can be safely and above all very easy to handle, attached to the jacket. A bearing is very precisely possible with the pull-out wire rope.

Console mount

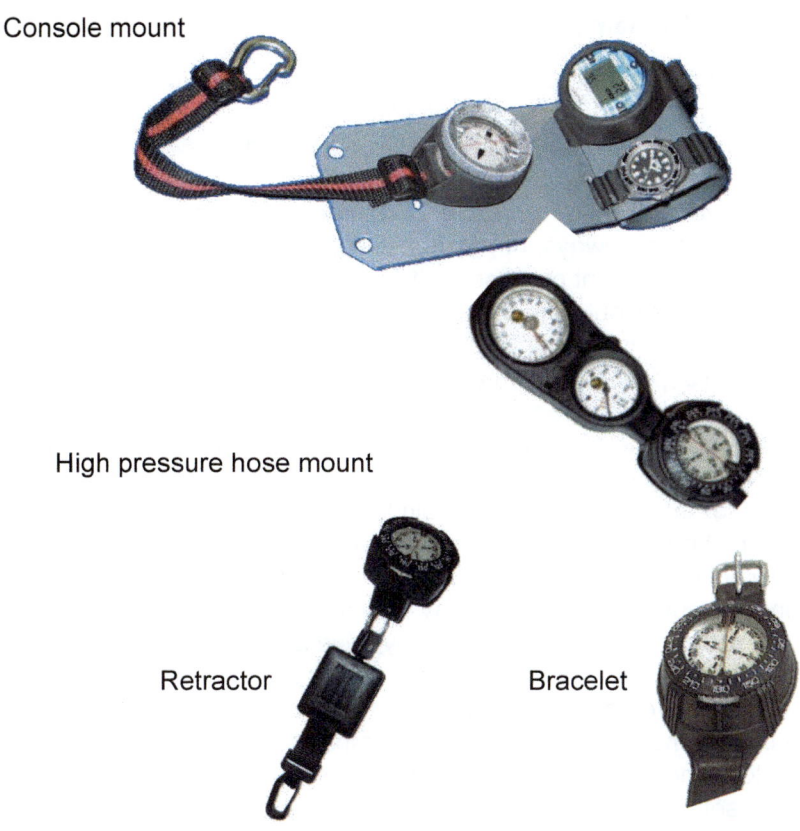

High pressure hose mount

Retractor   Bracelet

The care of the compass is similar to the care of other utensils, such as clock, depth gauge and regulator. Rinse well and then store dry and cool. The best way to learn how to use the compass is to take part in an appropriate course, as the underwater orientation has got a few challenges that you do not have on land, for example lateral displacement due to current.

2.7 The UW-lamp / torch

If there is a lot of sediment, plankton or other suspended particles in the water, you can switch off your UW lamp. The light is strongly reflected on the sediments, so that the view is usually worse after switching on the lamp than before. But, of course, if you dive by night or in a cave for example, you need a lamp. The options is, as always, huge. Just assume that there will be a lot of lamps for different purposes fulfilling your requirements. Therefore, I would like to give you no recommendations, please contact your instructor or dive shop; they will help you discussing several aspects about what to use best for your request. If you dive at night or in sea caves, you need at least two UW lamps, a main lamp and a reserve lamp. The reserve lamp can be small and of lower luminosity than your main lamp, as you only use its light for the return trip if the main lamp should have failed. This lamp should stay always in the pocket of your jacket, so you can always bring light into the dark. Maintain the lamp like all other instruments and especially pay attention to the state of charge of the battery. Most UW lamps today have an automatic charger and can always stay connected to the power point until they are used. However, you must pay close attention to one thing with your lamp, namely the seal (s). Some lamps need to be screwed apart to load the accumulator and then the seal is exposed. When you reassemble the lamp after charging, it is important that the gasket is completely clean and lightly greased. So-called O-ring or silicone grease you get in any well-stocked dive shop. Take very little of the grease, otherwise it may happen that sand or other particles combine with the grease and you then have to clean the seal and grease again. In addition, it is not so easy to get the grease off the fingers, as it is not soluble in water and even normal soap survives almost harmless.

Main lamp 20 to 100 Watt or, if needed, even more

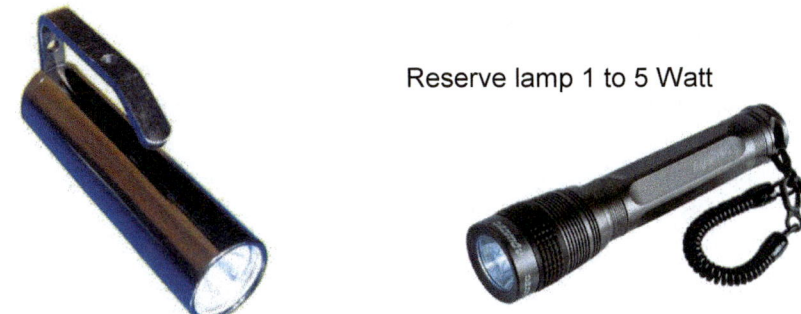

Reserve lamp 1 to 5 Watt

Main lamp with Accutank, 20 to ... Watt

Reserve lamp with SOS flash

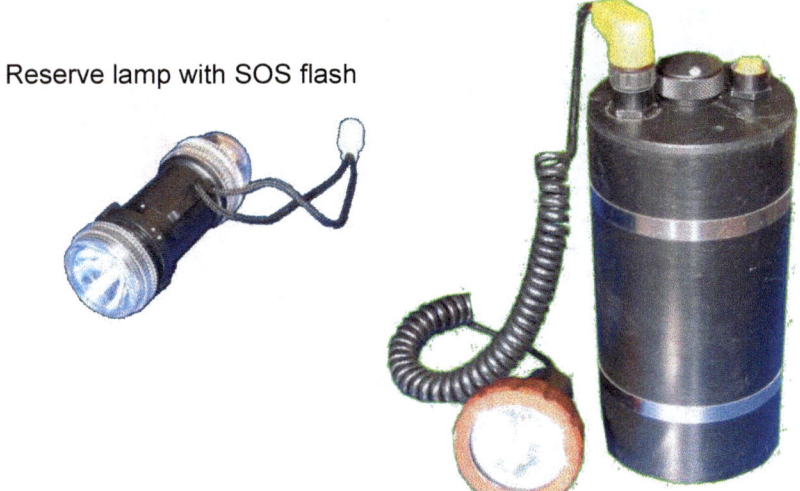

2.8 Safety equipment

No matter how well you plan and prepare for your dive, it might always be possible that something happens that you did not expect. This is in the nature of things and can happen to you in any other sport too. It is always good to have equipment in this case that can help to survive this emergency unscathed.

An example might be; you realize after surfacing that your boat has been set off alone, because a knot to anchor the boat has not been so well. In such case, it is nice if you can draw attention to yourself. At night light signals are suitable which other water sports enthusiasts or commercial boaters can see.

SOS flash and little lamp

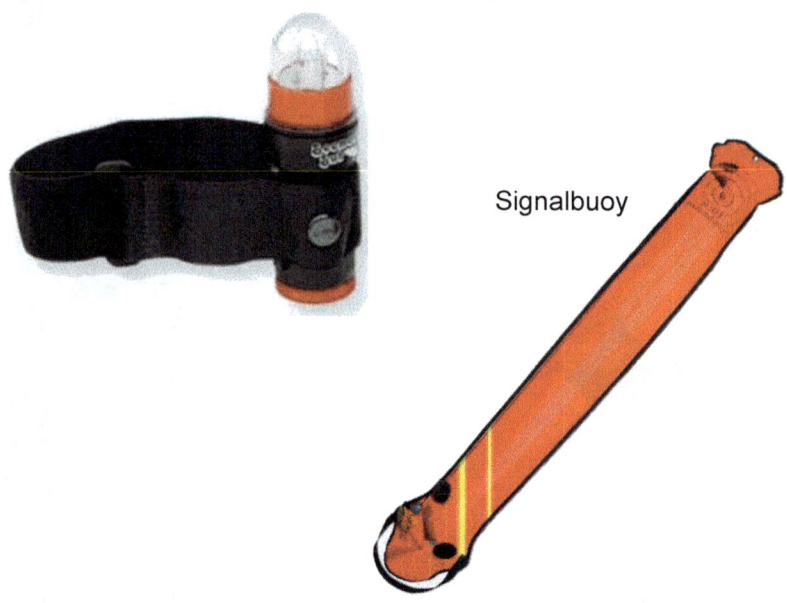

Signalbuoy

On the presentation of the glow sticks (cyalume) I renounce here for environmental reasons, although these sticks like to find use in diving and fishing. Many high-quality diving lights have an integrated SOS function, which means that they automatically send out the corresponding light pulses when requested by the diver. (SOS = three times short, three times long und again three times short). You can avoid all this, if you connect your boat neatly with the anchor. As a boatman the Palstek is certainly known to you. Here again as a reminder.

The Palstek is a non-tightening loop, so

the diving knot par excellence. All safety knots and loops

are made with the Palstek.

If, contrary to expectations, you have managed to sustain a diving accident, then you will be very happy if, in addition to plasters, iodine and bandages, you also have an oxygen kit on board or, in the case your dive started from the shore, in your car. Again, there are different systems, but they all have something in common; they are not cheap.

The most well-known systems are manufactured by the company Wenoll, the company Dräger or the American system DAN (Divers Alert Network). If you only dive under the supervision of a diving instructor, you can confidently leave this cost factor to the instructor or his staff, because they are required to provide oxygen for an accident.

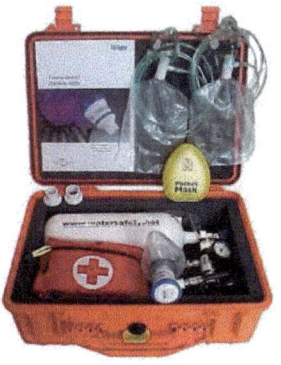

Example (with friendly permission of Dräger GmbH)

Medical oxygen is a drug that only a doctor may give. That is "in principle" correct. But "German" courts have judged that in the presence of an emergency, the so-called "justifying emergency case" exists (§ 34 StGB, only in Germany) and anyone who has received a briefing in the oxygen system, may give oxygen and even must (otherwise possibly § 323 c StGB, failure to provide assistance, too)! Please check your local laws and rules.

So, as with normal first aid, you are trying to save lives and prepare yourself through appropriate courses. If your last first aid course was just to receive your driver's license many years ago, you should urgently take action now. It could also hit your loved ones, and you would blame yourself all your life if, for fear of making mistakes, you did nothing to save lives.

2.9 More about the tank

Basically, there are tanks that are designed for 200 bar, 232 bar or 300 bar maximum operating pressure. They are mostly made of steel, but there are also tanks of aluminum or even composite materials which are mainly used for military purpose.

Tank with double valve

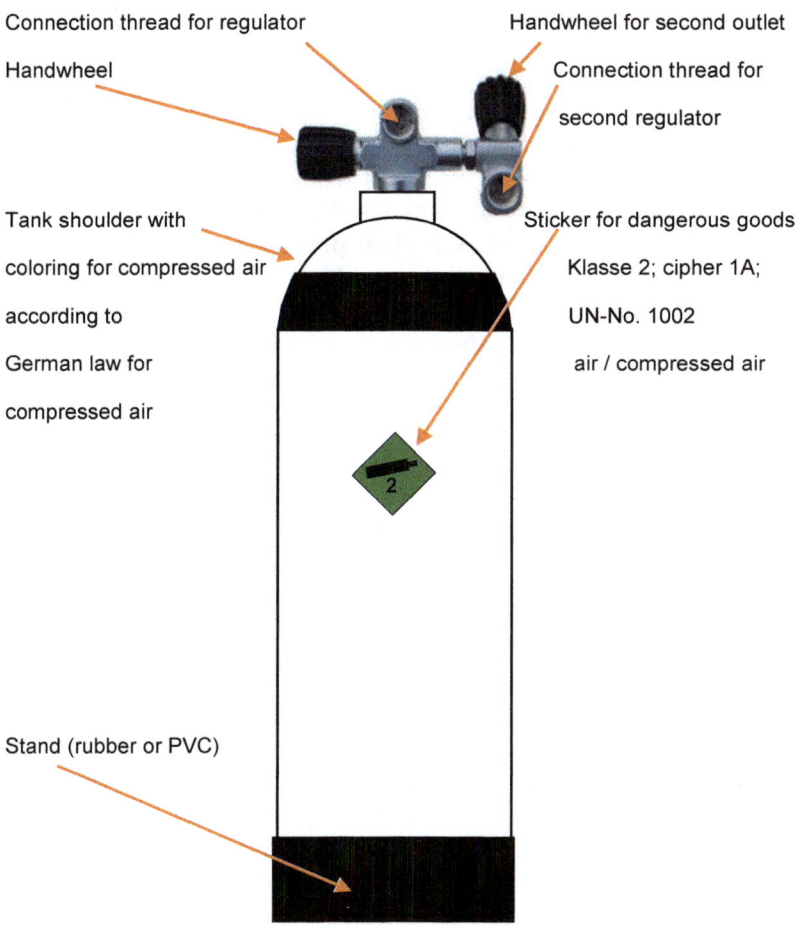

Connection thread for regulator

Handwheel

Handwheel for second outlet

Connection thread for second regulator

Tank shoulder with coloring for compressed air according to German law for compressed air

Sticker for dangerous goods Klasse 2; cipher 1A; UN-No. 1002 air / compressed air

Stand (rubber or PVC)

These tanks are available in many different sizes, each adapted to their use. Starting at 0.4 liter volume and ending (for recreational divers) at 20 liter, there is almost every volume size. The standard tank has a volume of 10 liter, but 12 or 15 liter are also quite common.

For divers who like to stay under water for longer, you can also combine the diving tanks into double packages, which are then connected with a so-called bridge. To avoid the tanks to bursts, because they are weakened by rust, they have to be checked regularly. In Germany, this is usually done by the TÜV (Technischer Überwachungs Verein – Technical Monitoring agency). Similar to the TÜV sticker on the license plate of a car in Germany, there are stickers (more recently) or hammered impact stamps on the shoulder of the tanks. Tanks can be in operation for decades with a little maintenance. **On the tank shoulder is next to the TÜV entry also the test pressure (50% above the maximum filling pressure), the working pressure or filling pressure (200, 232 or 300 bar), the date of the next necessary review, the tare weight, the volume of the tank and the nomination of the tank thread to mount the valve.**

The type of use as diving equipment (TG in German - Tauchgerät-) or breathing apparatus (AG – Atemgerät-) is also indicated. These are the most important entries for us. You may not dive with an AG it is only used, for artificial respiration on land, e. g. in an emergency case.

In Germany the diving tanks has to be checked by the TÜV every 2.5 years. And the tanks will be marked after inspection and weight check with a TÜV stamp. Every 2.5 years the TÜV marked the tank with an "I" (for inspection) or after a pressure test with an "F" (strength test). Your instructor can tell you how these exams are handled in your country. These tests alternate every two and a half years, so they are recurring as at our car. A tank in operation is always placed horizontally in order to avoid accidents, except you work at your equipment before or after the dive. However, if the tank is to be stored for a longer period of time, it should be stored upright and secured against falling over. Since a certain rust formation in the steel tanks cannot be avoided and the possibly condensed water always accumulates at the bottom of the tank, the upright storage makes sense, since the tank bottom is thicker than the wall due to production. If you transport your tank in the car, be

70

sure to secure the tank against rolling away or slipping. Bear in mind that you are essentially carrying a "bomb" that can release a very large amount of air in a very short period of time if damaged. Due to improper storage in the car, many coupes have already turned into a cabriolet in the event of an accident.

Always open and close the valves carefully and without force, otherwise parts of the valve, so-called spindles, may be damaged. Always open the valve completely before diving and then close it by about a quarter turn again. This is the only way to ensure the breathing air supply even at greater depths and your partner will recognize the opening degree of the valve during the partner check. Never completely empty the tank, otherwise water may penetrate and massively promote rust formation. Clean the valves after each dive with a lint-free cloth, toilet paper or kitchen paper. The unfortunately popular "ripping" of the valve to remove the water from the thread through the outflowing air is an ordeal for the environment and your ears, so you should omit this type of valve drying. Protect the thread with a blind plug against damage and contamination. The blind plug should only be screwed in hand tight and if possible have a hole (about 1 mm) to allow any pressure to escape. If you tighten this blind plug tightly and the valve is leaking or accidentally turned up a little bit, the blind plug will either be bombproof or it will fly around, depending on the material of the plug. If the plug is made of metal and the pressure has built up behind it, it is almost impossible to remove it without destroying it. Therefore, I take out the O-ring seal of the blind plug and thus cannot build up pressure. The valves of the tanks are today almost made of brass and are hard chromed to avoid tarnishing and oxidation.

Hand wheels to open and close the valve

Regulator connection 5/8"

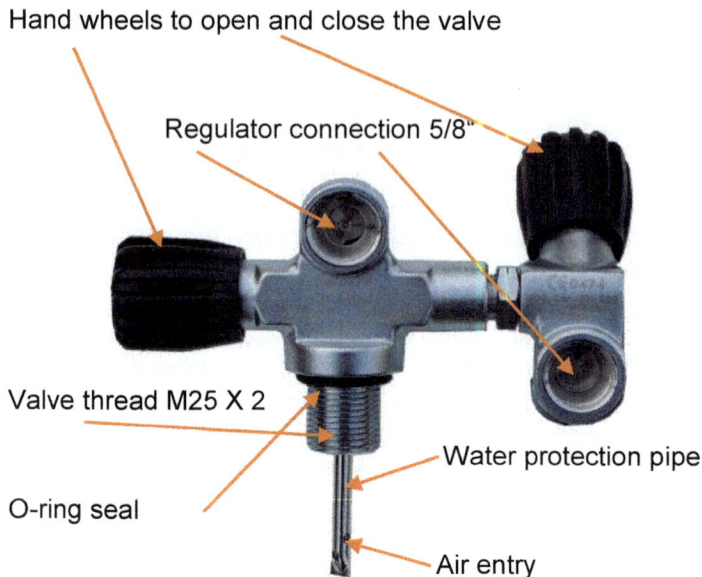

Valve thread M25 X 2

O-ring seal

Water protection pipe

Air entry

All work around the valve is best left to your instructor or the dive shop of your choice. It requires care and expertise to avoid mistakes that could end seriously bad. The water protection pipe should not protect the water of course, but protect the first stage of the regulator against the ingress of condensation when diving upside down.

2.10 More about the regulator

The high pressure gauge (also called Finimeter) at the end of a flexible hose, displays the current tank pressure. The dial and the pointer should, just like the Watch and the depth gauge, be luminescent and also have a colored marking for the beginning of the 50 bar range.

The glass should actually be made of glass and not, as with "cheap" products, made of plastic. This scratched very fast and makes a reading hard.

1. Stage

Medium pressure hose

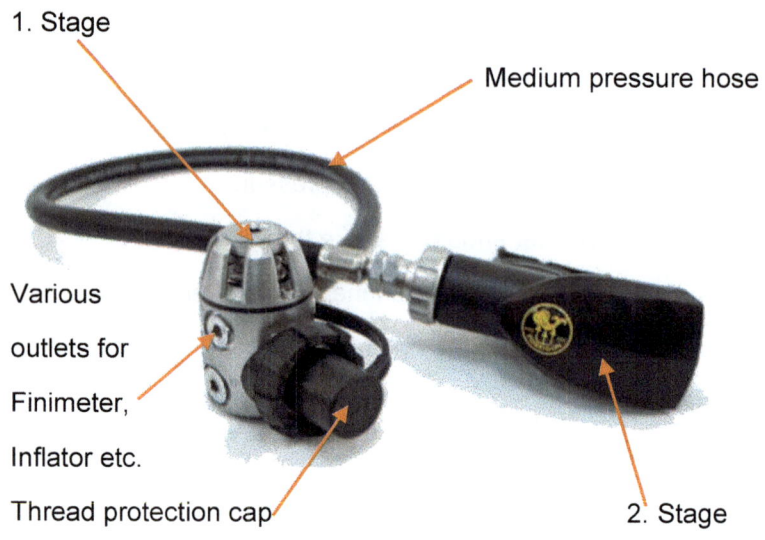

Various outlets for Finimeter, Inflator etc.

Thread protection cap

2. Stage

As already mentioned in the chapter Introductory Dive, such a regulator today consists of three parts. The first stage, which serves as a pressure reducer which reduces the tank pressure to a working or medium pressure, and the second stage, which is, strictly speaking, the actual regulator. Both stages are connected together by the third part, the medium pressure hose. The first stage has several medium pressure and one to two high pressure outlets. The second stages are operated at the medium pressure outlets and these outlets supply the air for the jacket and the drysuit too. The pressure gauge and, if present, the wireless pressure sensor for the diver's computer are connected to the high pressure outlets. So that these outlets cannot be confused, they have different thread sizes. 3/8 " thread for low pressure and 7/16" thread for high pressure. In addition, a reduction hole is attached to the high-pressure outlets, which ensures that even when the high pressure hose bursts only a maximum of 48 liters per minute can escape. Depending on the manufacturer, the first stages of the regulators have different working pressures. From 5 to 15 bar, just about every pressure is common. These pressures are design-related and are set by the manufacturer. If a regulator has a working pressure of 5 bar, it would theoretically mean that it delivers no more air at a water depth of 40 meters. To prevent this from happening, the first stages have a mechanism that ensures that the water pressure increases the working pressure of the first stage linearly. Thus, our first stage at 40 meters water depth would have a working pressure of 9 bar and a smooth breathing would be guaranteed. In the first stage, the tank pressure is reduced from 200 bar to the working pressure in one step. And since the gentlemen Joule (James Prescott Joule, British physicist, 1818 to 1889) and Thomson (William Thomson, British physicist, 1824 to 1907) have found that gases that relax at a nozzle, takes the necessary energy to escape out of the environment and generate cold thereby, the first stage is cooled down while breathing from the regulator. This process of refrigeration is named after the gentlemen mentioned above, Joule-Thomson effect. Now you may be wondering, why is he telling me this? Because this Joule Thomson effect can spoil your dive! It can always happen that one or two droplets of water creep into the first stage. Either because you did not press the thumb firmly enough to the first-stage high-pressure inlet when flushing the first stage, or because the compressor operator did not take his duty serious enough and the air drying system of the compressor has failed. If, therefore, the droplet in the first stage encounters the cold of the expanding gas, it will freeze and impair the function of the first stage. As a rule, your regulator, so the second stage, will blow off in an uncontrolled manner until the tank is empty or until your partner closes the valve of your scuba tank. Due to the frozen water in the first stage, this can no longer close and the medium pressure increases until the second stage, due to the design, opens and discharges the outflowing air into the water. This process is called internal icing. Stay calm in such a case and give your partner the sign "out of air" if he has not already noticed it himself. Then take your partner's octopus regulator, which he has already offered you of course, and finish the dive together. After this experience, bring your regulator and your tank to your trusted dealer and tell them what happened. He can then look in your tank and see if it contains moisture. He will inspect your regulator and, if necessary, dry it. Similar to the internal icing, there is the outer icing, which has nothing to do with moisture in the tank or the first stage but still ensures that your second stage blows off. Similar to the internal icing, there is the outer icing, which has nothing to do with moisture in the tank or the first stage but still ensures that your second stage blows off. Protective caps, which are offered by most manufacturers of regulators, are available against external icing. Ask the instructor and the stockist you trust. There are regulators whose tolerance to icing is very high and those that freeze faster. The first stages of regulators are controlled either by membranes or by pistons. In general, the membrane-controlled regulator is not only more expensive but also better protected against internal icing. Let advise you.

3. Diving medicine

A long time ago we were all fish or at least some creepy-crawlies in the ocean. But, what does a well-known diving equipment company say?

Evolution made us step out of the ocean – XXX helped us back again.

Nicely said and hits the core. Because, without such equipment we would make a rather pitiful figure underwater, at least after a few minutes. May it be the cold, the lack of air, or the high pressure. Something will try to spoil us the fun of diving. But, because we have learned a lot during the decades, we can dive today for a very long time and, if necessary, very deep, without dying or getting sick. And we owe this not only to the manufacturers of the diving equipment, but especially to the doctors and researchers who have dealt with the topic of man and pressure and cold. In this chapter, I will try to bring you closer to these aspects without getting bored.

3.1 The barotrauma

At the beginning of my remarks, in the introductory chapter, I mentioned the word Barotrauma and briefly explained it. Barotrauma always occurs when there are pressure differences during the dive.

Baro stands for heaviness, weight or pressure.

Trauma is injury or lesion.

Here is a medical phrase that ultimately says nothing else, but is a little more informative:

A barotrauma is an organ or tissue - specific injury to air - filled, rigid - walled or flexible body cavities due to lacking or insufficient ventilation with simultaneous change of the ambient pressure and a resulting difference between internal and external pressure

So, damage by pressure difference! Please remember!

Each one of us understands that the pressure changes permanently during a dive, because as the depth of the water changes, so does the pressure on our body.

Below is a small sketch that shows the three different phases of a dive and any damage that may occur. Before you start thinking about whether golf might not be more appropriate, I would like to assure you that 99.99% of all dives that take place are accident-free and that, as a rule, the human factor is mostly responsible for an accident.

Carelessness, ignorance and routine usually lead to accidents.

Hundreds of thousands of accident-free dives are performed every year, and if you maintain a healthy sense of skepticism and common sense and follow the contents of this book a little, you as a diver will enjoy diving for many years, and will (hopefully) die one day in your bed.

The phases of a dive and the specific diseases!

An ideal diving profile!

Compression phase (phase with increasing pressure)

Decompression phase (phase with decreasing pressure)

Isopression phase (phase with constant pressure)

During the compression phase can the following barotraumas occure:

Lung (especially during (too) deep apnea diving or snorkeling (snorkel length?)

Ear (mistake during the pressure equalization)

Head caves (mistake during the pressure equalization or colds)

Face and eyes (mistake during the pressure equalization in the mask)

Skin (too tight diving suit)

Teeth (fear of the dentist, like me ☹)

If we look at the words in parentheses, we quickly see that barotraumas in the isopression phase only occur if we make a mistake. For anyone who dives despite a cold or believes that his diving suit of 10 years ago is still fitting today, makes a mistake or suffers from false self-perception.

During the isopression phase can the following barotraumas occure:

If you have avoided all the above mentioned errors during descent, no new barotrauma can occur during this phase because the pressure does not change. However, if you change the depth during the "isopression phase", which is normal, we call this phase "variopression phase" (phase of changing pressure). This phase consists of many compression and decompression phases with the above mentioned possibilities of originating barotraumas. Pay attention to the pressure balance in the middle ear and the mask and if you feel well, just enjoy the dive.

During the decompression phase can the following barotraumas occur:

Lung (deficient or omitted exhalation during a rapid ascent)

Ear or head caves (when dived with a cold or mucous membrane decongestants. Many nasal sprays, which allow the mucous membranes to decongest, lose part of their effect when they are cold or mixed with water and the mucous membranes can swell up again.

Digestive organs (bowel problems with flatulence, no opulent meals before diving)

Teeth (with defective filling or crowns)

The conclusion that we can draw from the above-mentioned possibilities of creating a barotrauma is that if we dive carefully and pay attention to ourselves and the reactions of our body, nothing can happen in any of these phases. If the suit squeezes and hurts in the popliteal fossa (popular place), the suit is too tight and it needs to be replaced. If we do not get pressure equalization during the descent, we stop the dive and try again the next day. If it does not work then we will go to a doctor. If it pulls in your teeth when you are going up or down, it is likely that an old filling is not sitting well and you have to visit a dentist. Never force a pressure equalization by massive pressing or prolonged pressing; It can harm your body. Even a too tight hood can cause a barotrauma of the eardrum, so make sure that the surrounding water can reach your ears. If necessary, make some small holes (1 to 2mm) in the hood with a glowing knitting needle or a soldering iron around the ears. **But please remove the hood before!** Or you ask your instructor to do this for you if you are unsure.

And if we're smart enough to dive at home too to be fit on vacation, we've already checked these issues out and can look forward to beautiful dives. By the way, a quarry lake or a big pond has its charms too.

In order to be able to suffer from a barotrauma at all, in most cases, the breathing air is required.

3.2 The breathing and essouflement

Breathing is something unconscious. If we had to admonish ourselves constantly to breathe, we would start at the latest shortly after falling asleep the last step. So that does not happen, has God or the evolution created a system that works independently and, at least in the normal case, requires no intervention on our part. Now we divers are, as far as this system is concerned, special cases. Some of us breathe terrific amounts of air in and out to optimize the apnea (ancient Greek for respiratory arrest or breath holding) distance underwater, thereby completely upsetting the system. Others, in apnea, dive as deep as no rational fish would, and thus mess up not only the system, but also the pressure conditions in the upper body. A few divers also tend to save air to proudly show everyone else the finimeter after surfacing, to make it clear who this "top dog" is. That these air savers usually get a very severe headache and, when exaggerating, can even collapse, usually do not say or know it. Our breathing is a control system that is essentially determined by the carbon dioxide we exhale. Not by the vital oxygen, as you might imagine.

Our breathing air, which surrounds us all, consists of 21% oxygen (O_2), 78% nitrogen (N) and 1% residual gases such as argon, xenon, water vapor and a little carbon dioxide (CO_2) (0.04%) %). Since these residual gases, similar to nitrogen, in their low concentration have no influence on our body, we add them, purely by calculation, to the nitrogen. So we always calculate with 79% nitrogen. Nitrogen is a so-called inert gas, which we do not actually need, but since we can only change the atmospheric composition of the air by significantly more pollution, which of course we all do our best to do, we have to live with the nitrogen. If you read the term partial pressure, this refers to the proportionate gas pressure of the individual gas in the total pressure (Dalton law). In our air, the 100% gas pressure is 1 bar. The oxygen is involved with 21% of the total pressure so 0.21 bar oxygen partial pressure, the nitrogen to 79%, so 0.79 bar nitrogen partial pressure. Adding these pressures, we get back the total pressure of one bar. I am only telling you this because you should know that it is the specific gas pressure that gives a gas a narcotic or even poisonous effect. These pressures increase with increasing water depth. Calculations are required but only in the continuing diving courses. And pay attention to how often in the press, radio and television is spoken of oxygen cylinder, when actually meant an air-filled scuba tank.

The inhalation

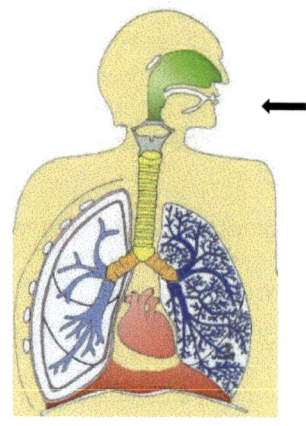

Rounded we inhale

21 % Oxygen (partial pressure 0.21 bar)

and

79 % Nitrogen (partial pressure 0.79bar)

The exhalation

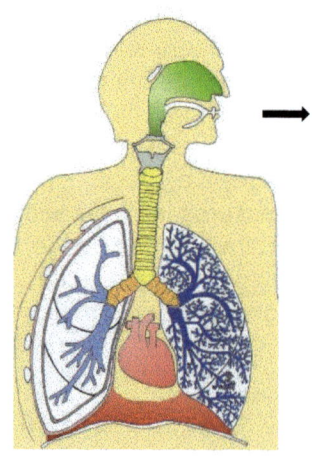

Rounded we exhale

17 % Oxygen (partial pressure 0.17 bar)

and

79 % Nitrogen (0.79 bar partial pressure)

und

4 % Carbon dioxide (0,04 bar partial

pressure)

If we compare the numbers, we find that we exhale 4% less oxygen, but exhale 4% carbon dioxide. Our body uses only 4% of the inhaled oxygen to maintain its functions. These consumed 4% are then exhaled as exhaust gas in the form of carbon dioxide. Thus, there are 3 different types of gas that we need to keep in mind as the training progresses.

Oxygen O_2 - Vital to us, as it is our most important "fuel".

Nitrogen N – A gas that we do not need to live but have to accept.

Carbon dioxide CO_2 – Vital as it controls the breathing.

Why carbon dioxide and not oxygen control our breathing is probably due to evolution, as the atmospheric oxygen content has changed dramatically over the millions of years. But that's just a guess, and ultimately it does not matter because we cannot change it. A network of nerves called the medulla oblangata, which forms the farthest and lowest part of our brain, just above the beginning of the spine, controls our breathing and uses the carbonic acid level in our blood as a clue. As already mentioned at the beginning, our body consists predominantly of water and carbon dioxide dissolved in water is called carbonic acid. We all know it from the mineral water or from the sparkling wine. The bubbles bubbling over there are nothing but dissolved carbon dioxide. The medulla oblangata thus holds its "feelers" in our blood and permanently measures the level of carbonic acid in the blood. Simply put, the medulla starts exhaling, depending on the level of carbon dioxide in the blood. The exhalation and the subsequent inhalation decrease the carbon dioxide content in our blood and the medulla is satisfied and unemployed for the moment. But now we live on and consume the just taken up oxygen again and produce again carbon dioxide, which turns again in our blood into carbonic acid. This gets the medulla again and ensures a renewed change of breathing gas. This control process is constantly repeated and thus keeps us alive. Now, over the course of millions of years, our entire system of gas uptake and delivery has been adapted exactly to us and our immediate living conditions. So we are optimized for life on land and at sea level. But we humans are discoverers and inventors and therefore nothing prevents us from trying the extreme. We climb high mountains and collapse there often, because the air is getting thinner and the oxygen content is getting smaller and smaller. We dive into the depths, although we are not build for that. But who does not dare, does not win. So we go everywhere even where we really should not be. But that's exactly what makes the charm, right? When we descend, the ambient pressure rises and burdens our body. If we do not have a marvel of technology, the regulator, our aquatic excursion would be over pretty soon. The regulator always gives us the air under ambient pressure, so that we hardly notice a difference to the surface. But, this difference exists and we can feel it with increasing water depth. As Boyle and Mariotte found out, the pressure under which our breathing gas must always be the same like the ambient pressure, otherwise we could not breathe. This means that, due to physics, our breathing air is compressed more and more with increasing depth and thus becomes "thicker", physically correct, denser. Our respiratory mechanics, i.e. the muscles needed for the inhalation and exhalation process, are optimized for the air density at the water surface and not for the 5 times higher density at 40 meters in the sea depth. And so, depending on the depth of the water, the muscles have to work harder and harder to get the "thick air" into our lungs and out again. This can lead to an overload of the respiratory muscles and thus to an insufficient ventilation of the lungs. Intensifying may be added psychological factors such as insecurity, stress or anxiety, as well as a too close fitting diving suit or a poorly maintained regulator. Due to the lack of ventilation, there is an increase in the carbon dioxide level in the blood and since this makes the inhalation signal, we begin to breathe intensified and start panting, but without causing a good ventilation of the lungs. This "out of breath" being is called in diver circles "essoufflement" and can lead in the worst case to powerlessness. If you experience such symptoms, immediately dive to a shallower depth, breathe deeply and consciously in and out, and if necessary, leave the water. To avoid this, it is best to wear only well-adapted equipment that gives you enough space to breathe freely and deeply. Plan the dive well and take the mental aspects into account and only dive if you feel completely fit. Then you are well prepared and an essoufflement cannot occur at all.

3.3 The depth intoxication / nitrogen narcosis / depth frenzy

Especially the gas, with which we could manage without, makes life as a diver the hardest: nitrogen. Since this gas is present in our breathing air to about 79%, it of course has the greatest potential to spoil us the dive. Experience told us, that from a certain ambient pressure in about 30 to 40 meter depth, nitrogen has a narcotic effect on us. This effect is called nitrogen narcosis or depth intoxication. The occurrence of this nitrogen narcosis is very individual and also dependent on the shape of the day. Are you tired, stressed or inexperienced, the depth intoxication can occur from a depth of 20 meters, the boundaries are fluent. On the other hand, there are professional divers who are able to handle compressed air far beyond the 40 meters, which is the considered limit for us scuba divers, and get no depth intoxication. The depth intoxication is similar to an alcohol frenzy, but who wants to be drunk in 40 meters water depth and almost be helpless? What might be relatively harmless in the pub can lead to accidents under water. With some of the following symptoms you can recognize the depth frenzy:

Metallic taste of the breathing air (often, not always)

Tube viewing (as if looking through a telescope, limited field of view)

If you now ignore these symptoms, the narcotic effect increases more and more with increasing water depth and the following effects on your body will occur.

Intoxication states with mental and physical performance limitations

Logical thinking decreases

Tasks will be completed incorrectly (e.g. underwater navigation)

Disturbances in fine motor skills

Hallucinations

This list could certainly continue, but the above symptoms should made it clear to you that a depth frenzy can be dangerous for you and your dive partner. So do not let it get that far, and stop the dive if you feel that your daily shape is not optimal. In order to determine a depth frenzy at the partner, one can arrange special hand signals before the dive, which require a little intellectual performance, this procedure is known from the technical and deep diving. For example, prior to the dive, you can ask your partner to respond to any OK sign with a triple OK sign or do similar "tasks". So you can see relatively well whether your partner is still capable of simple thinking. Your imagination got no bounds here.

3.4 Hyperventilation, pool blackout and shallow water blackout / ascent blackout

The multiple ventilation of the lungs, which is carried out over the need, i.e. the deep inhalation and exhalation often performed, is called hyperventilation. In medicine, the Greek or the Latin language has prevailed, and therefore we will come here even more often to such names. All of us once stood on the edge of a swimming pool and set our sights on creating the 25 or 50 meter dive in apnea, of course without the aid of a scuba tank. Therefore, we have tried to inhale as much oxygen as we can to reach our goal. Even when we would have known the risk we would take, we probably would have done it just the same. ☺ As a young person you feel indestructible. In addition, the success came, because we were able to dive after such multiple breathing in most cases longer as without. But the blood is always 95 to 100 percent saturated with oxygen. So it does not matter how often we inhale and exhale before our dive, we do not increase the oxygen content of the blood, possibly a little. That brings us at most one meter or two. Much more serious and therefore much more dangerous is that we exhale more carbon dioxide with our unnecessary multiple breathing and thus reduce the level of carbonic acid in our blood. Since this causes the respiratory stimulus much later, because we remember that the carbon dioxide controls our breathing, it can come to a powerlessness under water, because we still consume the oxygen out of our blood. So the oxygen is used up normally, but the respiratory reflex sets in late, maybe too late, because we have greatly reduced the carbonic acid content in our blood due to our hyperventilation. When the oxygen is consumed now, our body switches on the emergency system and all functions off that it does not necessarily need to survive. So the consciousness, the movement, the seeing, the hearing etc. This causes a powerlessness, which would force us, if we were not under water, just into the horizontal and let us wait there for help. But our brains do not know that we are underwater right now, perhaps it does not care about. It has its emergency program and this will be enforced.

Unfortunately, at this very moment, we find ourselves on the bottom of a swimming pool and would drown in short time if we did not get help. Hence the name of this very specific accident, namely **pool blackout**. Tip: tell somebody that you want to try to dive as far as possible and do not hyperventilate before!

You can breathe in and out two to three times deeply before you start your dive marathon, but no more. Freediving is a special part of scuba diving and requires good training and physical condition. Let your instructor advise you if you are interested.

What the distance for one is the depth for the other. The apnea divers worldwide try to always surpass the other in the reached depth. The world record is currently over 200 meters depth. The fact that they are in great danger and can do harm to their body is probably an aspect that makes the special appeal. The fact is that it has come several times to serious accidents in freediving. An apnea diver, who wanted to surpass his own record of 214 meters, is very seriously injured. Now we are certainly far from achieving such depths, but 20 to 30 meters are depths that a well-trained scuba diver can reach. So we are sitting in our boat and bobbing at anchor. Between us and the bottom of the sea are 25 meters of water, and on the bottom of the sea there is a dive weight, which we lost, because after our dive we have given our weight belt to somebody in the boat by holding the wrong side of the belt. And so this little piece of lead sank down to the bottom of the sea. My tip: let it be where it is, the next scuba diver is happy about it. But since you do not want to listen to me, you hyperventilate as prescribed two to three times and then make your way into the depths. The volume of your dive suit decreases, your weight belt pulls you down (slightly) and so the descent is a child's play (German saying). And, you hardly believe it, you reach the weight piece, grab it and swim back to the boat. What sounds like a success story may now become a drama. Of course, during your dive, you also used up oxygen that you took together with the breathing air from your lungs. At a depth of 25 meters, we have an ambient pressure of 3.5 bar, under which the oxygen stood. At the surface we have an ambient pressure of one bar, which is considerably less. During the ascent not only the ambient pressure, but also the partial pressure of oxygen decreases, which can lead to the brain activating the emergency program and what happens then, I have already explained under "pool blackout". But in this case 25 meters of water are beneath you and a rescue operation becomes very difficult, if not impossible. Especially if you did not observe the 50 bar reserve on your previous dive and none of your dive mates did, so no one got enough pressure on the tank to save you. This type of fainting is called **shallow water unconsciousness or ascent blackout** because it mostly occurs on the last 10 meters to the surface. Tip: Always make sure to maintain a 50 bar reserve and dive only as deep as you trained. In this specific case, a safety rope could have been a help. At the rope, your colleagues would have been able to get you on board. Not to mention that all the dive weights in the world is not worth a life.

3.5 The diving reflexes

A reflex is something that eludes our conscious control. There are many examples for this. If, for example, a mosquito or a wasp tries to crawl into our ear, we beat on the insect reflexive, without thinking.

Wikipedia (source) expresses it as follows: A reflex is an involuntary and rapid reaction of an organism to a certain stimulus.

Sounds more professional but means the same thing.

Of course, we divers also have all the reflexes that non-divers have, but two reflexes of it are particularly useful for us divers.

The Water-Nose Reflex

This reflex occurs when water enters our nose and touches the upper mucous membranes there. For example, when jumping into the water. This reflex triggers a respiratory lock to prevent water from entering the airways and drowning. This reflex is a bit annoying for us divers, as he can, for example, when removing the mask and the following blowing out of the mask, the breathing can affect so much that it comes to panic. Therefore, this reflex must be mastered by any diver. The good news is that this reflex can be "wracked out" over time. Sit in full equipment at 1.20 meters depth on the seabed (the head should be underwater), let the mask run full and put the mask back on properly. Now continue to breathe calmly with a mask full of water. Stay calm, because you can always get up and "save" yourself. It's best to have your dive partner with you who is keeping an eye on you. If you can do that, remove the mask completely and continue to breathe out of the regulator. If that works, you can try to dive smaller distances without a mask. So you slowly approach the diving without "nose lock" and train your water-nose reflex away.

The Dive-Reflex

Our past is in the sea, so mostly under water. As already mentioned, we all came out of the water millions of years ago. Some of our former buddies and friends stayed there and evolved underwater. We do not. Stayed in the water, I mean. Although one may well be divided on the second aspect, but that is not the content of this book. :-) But we have a reflex from the past time that we call today the diving reflex. This has been found out by the physiologist Paul Bert. The researchers are not quite sure what exactly causes this reflex, but it is believed that there are receptors (nerve endings) around the mouth and nose that signal to the body that we are above or below water. These signals and a few unexplained stimuli then tell the body that we are underwater and that we should stop breathing to avoid drowning. At the same time, our heartbeat slows down and the extremities (arms and legs) are less well supplied with blood. The physicians call this process centralization, because the body limits the vital functions and in extreme cases, only the core, the central is supplied with oxygen. It's all for survival, should we fall into the water. On the one hand a great thing, on the other not so nice, because we want to dive now and also have enough air to breathe. The good news is that we can reduce this reflex as well with a few training, and the reflex reduces during life too. So take your regulator and see how your body handles this reflex. Nothing can happen to you. In 99.9% of the cases, you will not notice much of this reflex, but you will find that you can relax underwater very well. If these reflexes did not exist, we would drown relatively quickly if we accidentally fall into the water.

3.6 The divers sickness (Caisson / decompression sickness)

You've certainly heard or read this term before. I can't explain why this disease deserves this name, as there are several diseases that can only happen to us divers if we are inattentive. But it is like that. The diving disease is also called Caisson's disease or simply caisson. Caisson comes from the French and means freely translated box. At the end of the 19th century, when the "Elbe Tunnel" was built in Hamburg, it was necessary to prepare the bottom of the Elbe for the foundations. For this purpose, large caissons were placed on the ground, weighted and filled with compressed air. The air squeezed out the water, at the same time ensuring that no new water could penetrate. Over sluices the workers were now send into the box and these could now prepare the ground for the foundations with shovel and hoe the whole day. Naturally, such work is difficult and demanding. Not only did this mean that the workers had to work under pressure for a long time, but also hard, which greatly increased their respiratory rate. So after a long day's work they were saturated under pressure with the gases of breathing air (Henry's Law). In short, gases like to dissolve in liquids. And the more so, the higher the ambient pressure and the longer the exposure time. Saturation occurs when under the current pressure no more gas can go into solution. This can go fast or take a long time, depending on pressure or gas type and respiratory rate. But at some point, the saturation occurs in any case. Now one can imagine that the workers were saturated after working hours of 10 hours and more at a water depth of 20 meters (3 bar). So they had the maximum amount of respiratory gas dissolved in your body, as it was possible in 20 meters of water. As good or as bad as in this case. At those days the doctors had no idea of the diving disease, because the diving medicine was still in its infancy. So the workers stopped their work and went to their favorite pub to have some drinks after work. At that time, the word "Feierabend" (German saying for the time after daily work) was taken literally, and if the wives did not collect the workers daily wage immediately after leaving the workplace, it was spent on drinks. That was on the Kiel shipyards, certainly also in Hamburg, until 1970 normal. Now the boys had made it to their pub and quickly consumed the first drinks, before they became dizzy and the joints began to itch. Since the life expectancy of a man in the 19th century was about 36 years, no one was worried too much when the eyesight disappeared for a few minutes, or the hearing did not really go along with it. In short, health was not the topic at the time. Thus, many workers managed to complete many of those working days. The more susceptible the workers were, the sooner they died. The more stable workers died a little later. And at those times nobody gave it really a thought. And at this time hardly anybody thought about it. But, apparently unnoticed by the public, in 1857 the German Felix Hoppe-Seyler had developed a theory of gas bubble embolism. Thus, it could have been known that the gases which the workers inhaled under high pressure and heavy labor and over a long period of time have been increasingly dissolved in their bodies. After leaving the caisson, however, the ambient pressure dropped massively, namely to 1 bar and thus the gas dissolved in the body escaped from the solution and formed gas bubbles exactly where it was at the time of pressure drop: so to speak all over. The blood circulation did the rest and flushed the bladders through the blood vessels until it came to accumulations (air embolisms), which obstructed the blood circulation or even completely stopped it. What can happen when parts of the body are no longer supplied with blood and thus no longer with oxygen, everyone can imagine. This state is called Caisson, but more precisely it is denoted by the abbreviations DCS 1 or DCS 2 where DCS stands for **dec**ompression **s**ickness. The numbers indicate only the severity of the disease.

In DCS 1, the main symptom is pain. Due to the accumulation of blisters, preferably at the bottlenecks of the vessels (veins), there is pain in the joints and appearances under the skin, such as redness and swelling. The bubbles that have formed are then often visible and palpable under the skin. The skin looks marbled and itches. The itching is referred to in the usage as "diver fleas". The pain in the joints caused by the blisters is called "bends". Because the pain especially in bending the joints occur.

The lymph nodes can also swell, but this is rarely the case. Already the type 1 of the DCS must be treated necessarily, also because he can change at any time in the type 2 ".

The DCS type 2 is the heavier case and already leads to failures in the neurological system of the body. To recognize:

Dizziness and / or vomiting

Muscle and joint pain already on appearance

Hearing, visual and speech disorders

Disturbed muscle coordination

Acute shortness of breath with chest pain, coughing and suffocation

Paralysis

Both cases must necessarily and very quickly get medical treatment, as it will be urgently necessary to bring the injured person back under pressure, which should be done in a professionally controlled pressure chamber at a hospital. Pressurizing this again, along with the administration of oxygen and medication, reduces the size of the bladders in the vessels and, ideally, the bladders can then be exhaled through the lungs

As a diver, who has detected a decompression accident, DCS 1 or DCS 2, to his dive partner, I act as follows:

Store the accident victim flat or if that is not feasible, sitting on the ground and leaning against a wall, a tree or the like

Give pure oxygen (100% O2) as long as possible

Provide fluid (water) when drinking is possible

Keep the injured person warm and avoid shocks

Mental care

Maintenance of vital signs (pulse and respiration), cardiopulmonary resuscitation if necessary

Alerting the rescue service (filling in the emergency card during the waiting period)

Enter the data of the dive on the emergency card and hand it, together with the computer of the injured person, over to the attending physician.

The data that must be entered on the emergency card is important to show the doctor the severity of the decompression accident, because the treatment also depends on how deep the victim has dived and how long he stayed at this depth.

However, you can easily avoid such a decompression accident by not diving too deep or staying too long in that depth. There are so-called decompression tables, from which you can take the times and thus are always on the safe side. If you then have a dive computer your own, it will show you in time when you should change the depth to avoid a "caisson".

Notice the term "NO-STOP TIME", this means the "no decompression limit"! No stop time is the time you can spend at a certain depth (pay attention, the descent time is part of it), **without** having to make a decompression break when surfacing. These times are, according to the depth of water, in the decompression table. The safest way is to dive always within the "No-Stop time" and at the end of each dive maintain a safety decompression stop of 3 minutes at 5 meters.

A decompression stop is always necessary if you have dived outside of no-stop time. Since you have in such a case particularly strongly saturated with breathing gas, that is, too much dissolved nitrogen in the blood, you must first exhale this nitrogen, before you have reached the water surface. This is done by ascending to a certain water depth, depending on the table or instructions of the dive computer, and waiting there until some of the nitrogen has been exhaled.

We call these breaks deco stops or decompression breaks. The depths that must be adhered to begin at 15 meters according to the table and then leading in 3-meter increments up to the surface. A computer calculates the decompression much more accurately and individually, but the table has no batteries and thus cannot fail during a dive. Tip: Even if you use a dive computer, like 95% of recreational divers worldwide now, always put a decompression table in the pocket of your jacket and always pay attention to your diving depth and your diving time. If your computer fails then, which luckily hardly ever happens, then you can do with the help of the decompression table a halfway usable decompression. In such a case, it is better to stay on a decompression break for too long rather than too short. Your dive partner may have a dive computer, and if you've dived like your partner, just stay together with him at the deco break. Remember, a good dive partner is the best life insurance we can have under water.

Hence our motto:

Never dive alone!

If you want to be on the safe side, always stay within no-stop time and make the safety decompression stop from 3 minutes to 5 meters. So you have done everything right and made a nice and safe dive. Apart from the sharks. (Joke, sorry, must be) ☺ But now I have to mention that more people die from a coconut that has fallen on their heads than from a shark attack. The shark is not a killer beast that really want to eat you. Mostly he wants to check the object his other senses told him about, realises a bubbling „fish" rather than a typical prey and disappears in the deep blue. Sometimes he might be curious and approaches you. However, if you want to dive with sharks, be sure to entrust yourself to a guided tour. The guide knows exactly where to look at sharks and recognizes immediately if a shark feels annoyed and might even want to chew a divers fin. Remember, we're just a guest underwater and have only a rough idea how life underwater is. But if you have found a treasure in 40 meters (although you should not go to this depth with your current level of training), which, understandably, you do not want to leave to the others, then you will certainly fall out the of no-stop time, as you dive pretty deep and stay there for a long time. For this water depth, the decompression table Deko 2000 from Bühlmann / Hahn indicates a no-stop time of 7 minutes. Assuming that it takes you 2 minutes to get to that depth, you only have 5 minutes to collect the gold on the spot. Depending on the size of the treasure this is not a long time. Especially since you will then probably be very excited, at least I would be, and thus generate an increased respiratory rate. However, this increased respiratory rate means that you are increasingly saturated, so more respiratory gases can go into solution, which means either a reduction of the no-stop time or an extension of the decompression times. So it is probably good that the treasures are rarely found under water and this "case" is a little far-fetched. Do not unnecessarily endanger your life by pushing the limits. At shallower depth, depending on the water, it is much brighter and the colors are still quite visible. There are much more interesting animals than on for example 40 meters. You can find great targets for your UW camera there and there is almost no risk of a decompression accident. For example, I can spend hours and hours in the Baltic Sea at 3 to 5 meters, where you can see shrimp, fish, crabs and starfish. Karen also. 😊

96

We were forgiven for the slightly shaky image, the crab was more important to us than the perfect buoyancy or posture, and since the sea ground were only a few meters below us, we could "sink" carelessly. And even if you do not believe it, we did not force the little crab to climb on Karen's arm. He had just decided to "jump" from the pier on which he had sought food on the seabed and landed on Karen's arm. You also have my word of honor that the animal has survived the filming completely unscathed.

As IDA or CMAS Diver *, Open Water Diver or Junior Open Water Diver, you should not do any dives outside the no-stop time. If you want to dive, find an experienced partner to accompany you. In order to make your choice of diving depth a little easier, here are some no-stop times.

Please note that the listed no-stop times also include your descent time. These values are valid for a height above sea level from 0 to 700m!

Depth	No-stop time
12 Meter	140 Minute
15 Meter	72 Minute
21 Meter	31 Minute
24 Meter	23 Minute
27 Meter	18 Minute
30 Meter	15 Minute
33 Meter	12 Minute
36 Meter	10 Minute
39 Meter	9 Minute

Scuba divers do not dive deeper than 40 meters! In some countries, such as Egypt, there is even a diving depth limit of 30 meters. With the beginning of the ascent, which must then be carried out continuously, the no-stop time ends, as the pressure now steadily decreases. This means that if, for example, starting the descent phase (starting with the head is underwater) and you reach the sea ground in 15 meters and start the ascent phase in less than 72 minutes, you are within no-stop time. Nevertheless, at the end of each dive you should make the 3 minutes safety stop at 5 meters depth.

However, if, contrary to expectations, you actually plan a decompression dive, you will find the exact procedure for how to use the deco table Deko 2000 in the appendix to this book. The decompression tables for dives up to 700 meters above sea level and from 700 meters above sea level you can order from IDA at K.Reimer@ida-worldwide.com.

3.7 The Rescue chain

As in a car crash, there are "life-saving immediate action" in diving, which every diver should master. As already mentioned, we are legally obliged to help an accident victim as far as we can, without endangering ourselves. Therefore, one of the most important aspects of scuba diving is first aid, and this aspect will face you in every new course that you will experience in your long and happy diving life. Even if this topic is not one of your favorite topics and you get a little queasy, if you see that you are a first responder. Do not worry, that's life and in this situation everyone feels like you. But it is much better if you are prepared for such a situation than standing in front of the injured person and not knowing what needs to be done. Nobody, not even a judge, will expect you to have the skills of a paramedic or a doctor, but you can certainly be expected to ventilate an injured person or perform a cardiac pressure massage, and you should also be able to put the victim in a stable lateral position. With us divers, then, in general, the giving of oxygen is added. And even if you do not dare to help the injured person, you can at least shout and look for help or call for help over the phone.

A helper needs to keep a clear head and should not act completely haphazardly. So the rescue operation starts with getting an overview and trying to stay calm (easy told, I know).

See - evaluate - act

If we have been bitten by an animal or injured by a stone or a coral, it is not necessarily a diving accident, even if it happened while diving. Of course, these wounds must be supplied. Even a heart attack, which unfortunately can occur in untrained divers, is not a diving accident, because this type of accident could just as well happen when cycling or playing football.

A diving accident depends causally on the increased pressure or the too rapid reduction of the pressure. So it comes either to a barotrauma or to a decompression accident. Depending on the severity of the accident, it may be necessary to pressurize the injured person again, i. e. to bring him into a decompression chamber. The so-called "wet recompression" is not a good idea, as an already injured diver under no circumstances may be brought underwater again. Call professionals for help and dial the rescue phone numbers you need to know in time, before an accident happens.

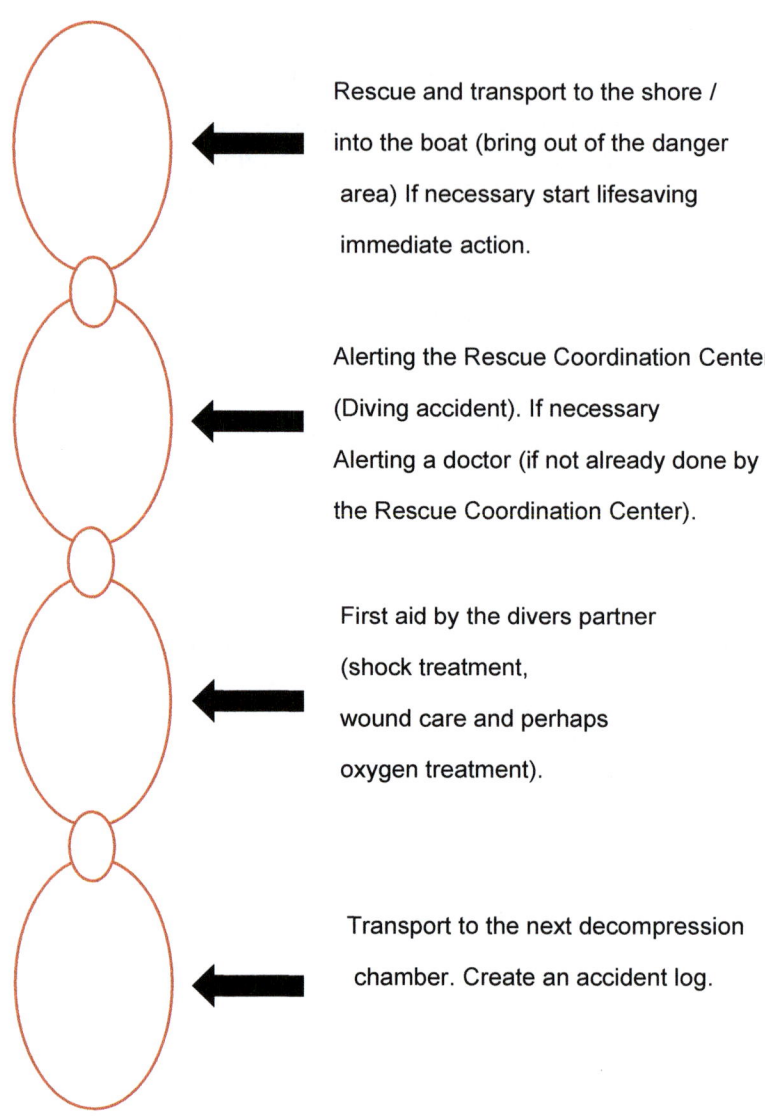

Rescue and transport to the shore / into the boat (bring out of the danger area) If necessary start lifesaving immediate action.

Alerting the Rescue Coordination Center (Diving accident). If necessary Alerting a doctor (if not already done by the Rescue Coordination Center).

First aid by the divers partner (shock treatment, wound care and perhaps oxygen treatment).

Transport to the next decompression chamber. Create an accident log.

Immediate action

Secure and rescue

Control of

Consciousness – Breathing – Pulse

Emergency call

Via handy, radio or landline

101

First aid

For example to create

a bandage

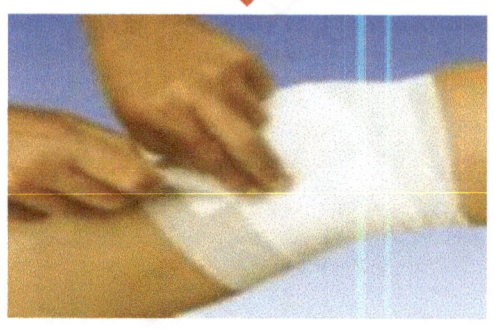

Rescue service

Transport to the hospital

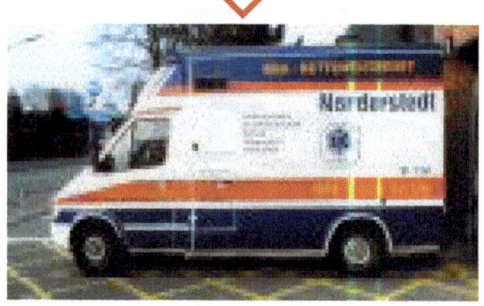

102

Hospital and / or

decompression chamber

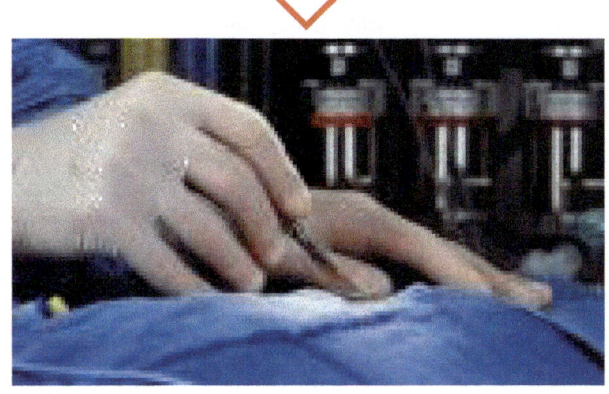

Schematic procedure if the injured person is open to conversation!

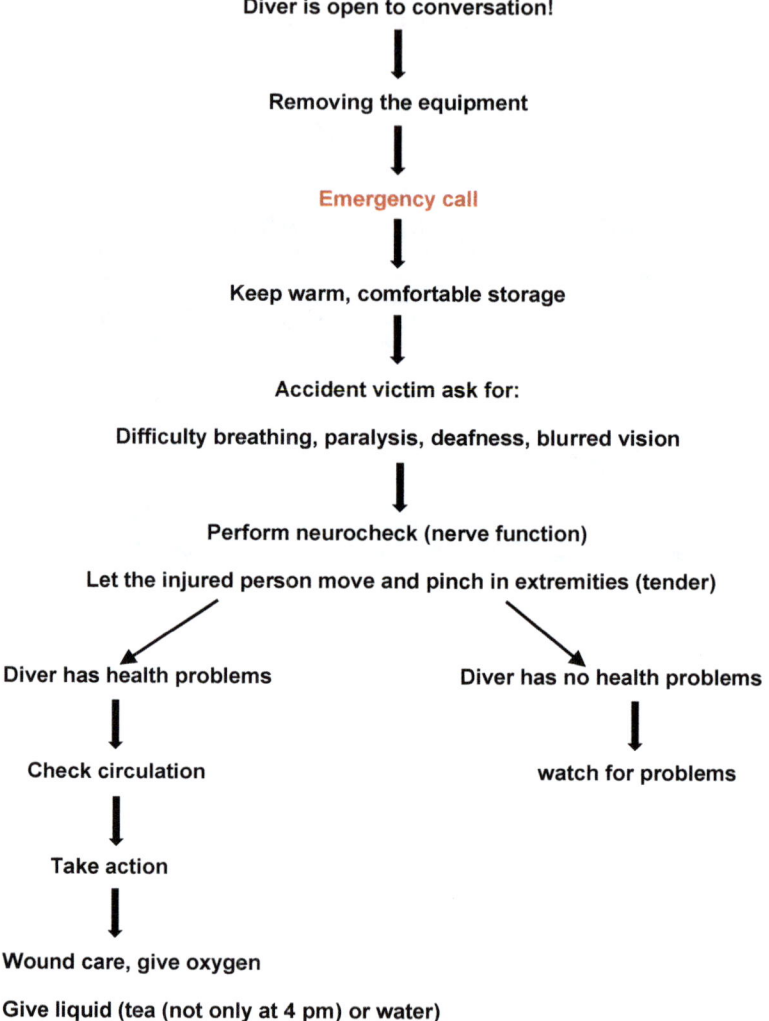

Diver is open to conversation!

↓

Removing the equipment

↓

Emergency call

↓

Keep warm, comfortable storage

↓

Accident victim ask for:

Difficulty breathing, paralysis, deafness, blurred vision

↓

Perform neurocheck (nerve function)

Let the injured person move and pinch in extremities (tender)

Diver has health problems

↓

Check circulation

↓

Take action

↓

Wound care, give oxygen

Give liquid (tea (not only at 4 pm) or water)

Diver has no health problems

↓

watch for problems

Schematic procedure if the injured person is <u>not</u> open to conversation!

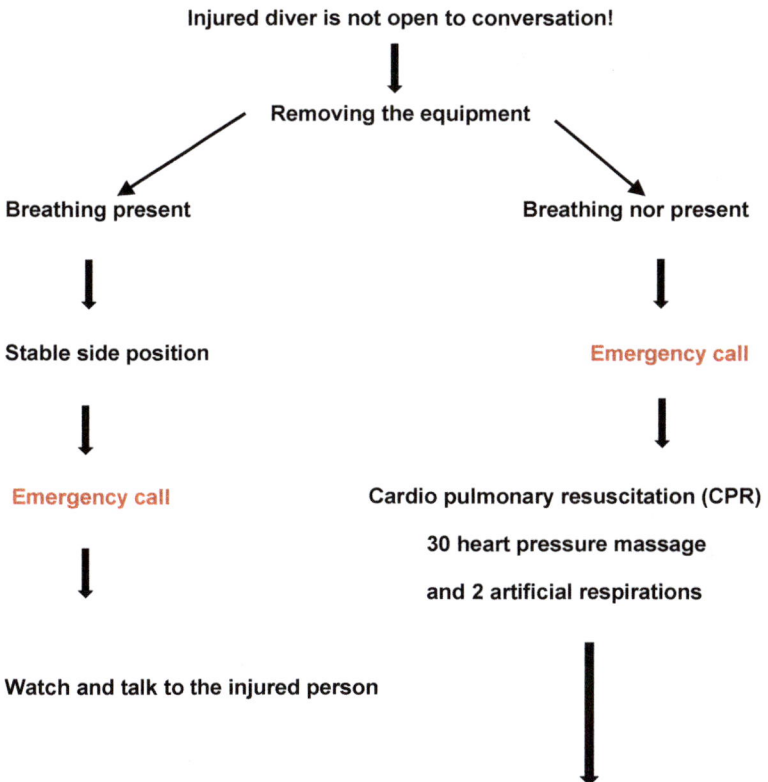

Injured diver is not open to conversation!

Removing the equipment

Breathing present

Breathing nor present

Stable side position

Emergency call

Emergency call

Cardio pulmonary resuscitation (CPR)

30 heart pressure massage

and 2 artificial respirations

Watch and talk to the injured person

Perform CPR until the doctor / paramedic takes over

or until there are clear and unmistakable signs of death.

A medical layman is not entitled to determine death.

The resuscitation must be practiced actively and intensively by each participant. For this purpose, a resuscitation model is absolutely necessary. The exercises and teaching content must follow the current guidelines of the European Resuscitation Council (ERC) or of the AHA (American Heart Association). As these guidelines may change, depending on medical progress, it makes sense to attend a first aid course every year.

3.8 Hypothermia and Hyperthermia (overheating)

Thermie reveals a little about what's coming now. Almost everyone has a water heater at home and this usually generates heat for the bath water and the heating system. So this is about heat or missing heat. The terms hypo- and hyper come from the Greek and are so-called "prefixes", ie word extensions that stand before the word stem, here Thermie. Hypo stands for "under", as in mortgage, which means that the money in our wallet is underrepresented. Therefore, we have to borrow something from the bank, for example, to pay for our house. Hyper stands for "more or over" and that can only be the fabled Hyperman, who, according to the comics of that time, was stronger than Superman. You see, I stay true to my donkey bridges (German saying for mnemonics). Thus, hypothermia means too little heat and hyperthermia too much heat. When does this happen to us? Very easily. Almost always. Those who are freezing already suffer from hypothermia and this can go so far that we to lose consciousness. Not recommended under water. If I am cold, I will end the dive immediately, because a freezing diver is a bad diver and can be a danger to his dive partners.

Core body temperature

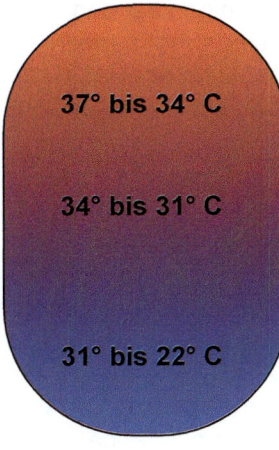

37° bis 34° C	1. Phase (defense) Muscel tremor, high heart rate, increased breathing
34° bis 31° C	2. Phase (exhaustion) indifference, fatigue, puls- and blood pressure drop, muscle rigidity, cardiac arrhythmia
31° bis 22° C	3. Phase (paralysis) apparent death, Reflex lotness, respiratory and cardiac arrest

But do not worry now, before all this happens, you are already voluntarily leaving the water because you shiver so much that you have no joy to dive further. But what if you now have a dive partner who still cannot stop diving (The Treasure, remember?) and continues, even though he already shows the signs of the first or second phase? Take the colleague literally by the hand and leave the water together with him. Make sure that the, let's call him casualty, depending on the severity of the hypothermia, immediately take off the diving suit and will be warmed up! Blankets and hot sugary drinks (no alcohol) are appropriate here. If the second stage does not make this treatment possible, immediately call the ambulance and keep the casualty warm until the doctor arrives. Also pay attention to the vital signs and resuscitate, if necessary. To avoid all this trouble, you should, according to the water temperature, stock up with suitable equipment. Such a dry suit is not a bargain, but freezing or possibly dying is much worse. For even the most sensitive, the scuba industry keeps even electric socks and vests ready for wearing under the suit. The opposite of freezing (hypothermia) is known to be sweating (hyperthermia). It's usually nice to keep it warm, but it can be too much of a good thing. Overheating of the body occurs when heat dissipation is disturbed. There can be different reasons. Unsuitable clothing and / or high heat and strong, often unfamiliar sunlight are the causes. What happens when the body overheats? Loss of fluids (sweating or even dehydration) not only causes us to lose water, but also to the lost of essential salts that the body desperately needs. Dehydration occurs when we sweat heavily and do not drink enough or also because of a diarrhea. The blood, which contains a large part of the water in the body, now becomes thicker and the flowability and the ability of the oxygen transport decreases. A heat exhaustion occurs, and if not reacted quickly by cooling and water supply, it comes to the next step, the heat-powerlessness. In such a case, according to the rescue chain shown above, must be react and the casualty must be cooled. Also the cooling must be done carefully, because a too large temperature difference in too short a time, can negatively affect the circulation of the casualty. If the casualty is responsive, give it water (with electrolytes such as potassium, magnesium, calcium, sodium) and bring it in the shade, preferably in a cool room (no cooling chamber). Elotrans® is a good supplier of electrolytes and is also recommended for diarrhea. You will get Elotrans® in every pharmacy and it should not be missing in any travel pharmacy. **But please talk to your family doctor before you take them because Elotrans® is not suitable for everyone and may even be harmful.** If you have nothing of the sort, a tank of mineral water is the best alternative, cold tea with plenty of sugar is also suitable. A good solution is water with salt and sugar. 1 liter of water mixed with one spoon salt and two spoons sugar. Salt for the minerals and sugar for the taste. If the casualty is unresponsive, bring him into a cool room or in the shade, if no building is accessible and call a doctor immediately. Free the casualty from clothing (diving suit) and monitor his vital signs. Reanimate, if necessary, until the doctor arrives. You can prevent hyperthermia by wearing appropriate clothing. So no dry suit with 9 mm neoprene strength in the Red Sea, but a 3-mm diving overalls, also to protect against injury. Avoid the blazing midday sun, stay in the shade and drink plenty of water. Also think of the electrolytes. But even when diving, we breathe in very dry air, because the compressor cleans and dries the air to prevent the rusting of the tanks. In addition, it is due to the horizontal position in the water and the higher ambient pressure to a higher urinary frequency (called diuresis). But please not directly into the suit, what is called divers heater and what is **disgusting**. Because the smell is hard to get out of the suit. In foreign countries, with unfamiliar nutrition, may also be added to diarrhea or vomiting, and we have a classic dehydration disease. Incidentally, it is true that electrolytes are also present in beer, but the alcohol in it is unfortunately counterproductive. So wait with the beer until you are well and fit again.

3.9 Diving and nutrition

Water is not only the element in which we prefer to move, it is also the element we mostly made of, namely about 70%. Much of this water is bound within the body cells but there is also a lot of water in the blood. Depending on the amount of water present in the blood, the blood is flowable or not. Since we want to get rid of the too much inhaled nitrogen as quickly as possible and the blood takes over the transport, we should be anxious that our blood is always flowable. So drink plenty of water, especially in warm areas, and be sure to replenish the minerals flushed out by sweating and any increased urination. The best is to talk to your family doctor before a dive trip and get tips from him. If you want to dive in the morning, prepare for it the night before. Drink little or better no alcohol and do not eat anything that could rob you of sweet sleep. Have a little breakfast before the dive and drink not more than one cup of coffee. But I've heard that the British like tea more than coffee. That's good, drink tea instead of coffee bevor you dive. Avoid anything that irritates your stomach unnecessarily, otherwise you might already loose during the boat trip the joy to dive. Also keep in mind that all gases in the body participate in pressure equalization. And there are always a few bladders in the gastrointestinal tract, which can cause pain due to the size change. Generally, avoid before diving any food or drink that may cause bloating before diving. Carbonated mineral water is not well suited, prefer to drink still water before diving. Do not eat legumes (peas, beans, lentils etc.) before the dive, not even the night before. Do not dive immediately after eating, but wait at least one to two hours before you go into the water. And last but not least, if you are not completely comfortable, stay ashore and do not dive.

3.10 Diving and drugs

Yes, alcohol is a drug too. What could be better than talk about the dive with your diving partners after the dive and have one or two beers? Only little but be reassured, that is an essential part of the "Aprés" and is also part of our sport and not just football. The human body is said to degrade about 0.1 per thousand alcohol per hour. So it certainly does not mind if you drink a "nightcap" in the form of a beer on the eve of the dive. But then it should stay with one beer, otherwise you increase the susceptibility of your body to a deep intoxication and also the tendency to decompression sickness intensifies. The best way to decide to dive or not the next day is to make the decision the day before and behave accordingly. I do not want to commend alcohol here, but it would be hypocritical not to mention the beer after diving and at the same time to "demonize" the smoker. Of course you can also drink tea, water or coffee for "Aprés". But it is, and this experience I have done in many countries of the world, not the same. For that I certainly get scolding, but almost 40 years of diving practice with "Aprés" have made me and no one I know a drinker or sick. Enjoy everything in moderation and how did Paracelsus say: "*All things are poison, and nothing is without poison; only the dose makes it that a thing is not a poison*" (source: wikipedia)

Now there are also drugs that can be smoked or that you have to inject or just swallow. As far as I know, there are no studies on their effects on scuba diving and therefore I strongly advise against diving after the "enjoyment" of these forms of drugs. Also medicine of whatever kind are ultimately drugs and since only a healthy diver should go into the water and a diver who takes medication is not healthy, by definition, should not go diving when taking medication. But.... There are medications that do not necessarily preclude diving and even a well-adjusted diabetic may dive. However, the jungle of diseases and medicines can only be understood by a specialist and therefore ask your doctor or pharmacist if you may dive despite taking "your" medication. Nicotine is also a drug and the effect of a cigarette on the human body is enormous and not completely describable here. A smoker has an increased risk of a lung overpressure barotrauma due to the constriction of the bronchi by the ingredients of the cigarette smoke. Cigarette smoke contains carbon monoxide too and this substance hinders oxygen uptake by the blood. In short, smoking is about the worst thing you can do to your body, both above and under water.

4. Diving physics

As you may have already noticed while reading this book, there are other topics besides dive medicine and diving equipment that should be considered. For example, the diving physics, which I would like to bring you a little closer here. Again, it is the pressure or pressure relief that keeps us busy.

4.1 The law of Henry (William Henry, English chemist 1774 – 1836)

Gases are able to dissolve in liquids. So the carbon dioxide turns into carbon acid, which makes our mineral water prickle so nicely and forces us to belch when the gas exits the solution due to the heat in the stomach, which is the case with all carbonated drinks. The solvent power of the gases depends on various factors. We deal primarily with three gases: oxygen, nitrogen and carbon dioxide. The following factors are very important as they greatly affect our underwater behavior.

Ambient pressure – The higher the ambient pressure under which we are, the better a gas can dissolve in us, more precisely in our body tissues. Our body is made up of many different tissues, which, according to your blood circulation, are divided into fast and slow tissues. Muscles are always on the move, need a lot of energy and are therefore well supplied with blood. They absorb the additional dissolved gases very quickly, but release them very quickly too. Fat and bones are less supplied with blood and absorb the gases very slowly, but they also give them off very slowly. The idea was to find a solution that would take into account all the tissues and thus enable an accident-free dive. These models have been developed by scientists and physicians and are used in decompression tables and dive computers.

Time – The longer we stay under pressure, so dive, the more gas dissolves in our body. Depending on the tissue type, slow or fast, a tissue will be saturated after a certain amount of time. This means that it cannot absorb more gases during this time and under this pressure.

Activity – The more we are active under water, the more gas dissolves in our body because the blood flow of each tissue type increases.

Temperature – The colder a liquid is, the more gas can dissolve in this liquid. This factor is not that important for us divers, but it should not be completely neglected, see time addition in extreme cold by using the decompression table.

When reading the above lines, it is clear to everyone that our breathing gases are increasingly dissolved in our bodies during diving, depending on pressure, time, temperature and effort. Therefore, it is essential to comply with the necessary decompression stops when surfacing, in order to allow the body to breathe off these gases before we reach the surface of the water.

4.2 The law of Archimedes

(Greek mathematician and physicist 287 to 212 (presumably) BC)

The law of Archimedes we have already met in the chapter "introductory dive" and nothing more to add. Of course, here we can talk shop, how far a diver would go down into mercury (not so deep at all) or in pure alcohol (pretty deep), such mind games are fun and explain the principle, but are not effective here.

4.3 The law of Boyle & Mariotte

(Robert Boyle 1661, Irish physicist and Edme Mariotte 1676, French physicist)

The law of Boyle Mariotte says something about the relationship between pressure and volume. Since gases can be compressed their volume naturally changes. Because what is compressed becomes smaller. To simplify matters, let's take a balloon that we have inflated on the surface and now has a volume of 2 liters. The pressure in the balloon is slightly above the ambient pressure of one bar, otherwise the rubber skin would not be so taut and it would not pop so nice when it bursts. Now we grab this balloon and go down with it, which requires a little power in the legs, but is feasible. As we submerge, the ambient pressure increases, as we have already learned. The gas in the balloon is now compressed so that there is always the same pressure inside the balloon as it is outside the balloon. When compressing the balloon gets smaller, but the pressure in the balloon rises. Now we have arrived at 10 meters water depth and find out there that the balloon has become considerably smaller and now also much easier to hold, as its buoyancy has decreased. Boyle and Mariotte have discovered that the balloon is now exactly half of the size which he had at the surface and that it has exactly twice the pressure he had at the surface. Namely the pressure that prevails at 10 meters water depth, ie 2 bar. From this they have made a formula that is there

P x V = C

P is for pressure. V is for volume and C is for constant

Thus, for a given amount of gas, the pressure is inversely proportional to the volume. If the pressure drops, the volume increases, if the pressure increases, the volume decreases. Just like with our balloon. Let's just let go of the balloon, it rises to the water surface. Now, the ambient pressure drops and the balloon grows back to its starting volume of 2 liters. To illustrate this process a bit, a picture.

Let's assume that our balloon has a volume of 10 liters.

That means according to the law of Boyle Mariotte's P x V = C

P is 1 bar   V is 10 liter   und C is the C as in Constant

So 1 bar x 10 liter is 10 barl (barliter, so bar x liter)

Depth	Ambient pressure	Volume	air quantity in barl
0m	1 bar	10 liter	10 barl
10 meter	2 bar	5 liter	10 barl
20 meter	3 bar	3,3 liter	10 barl
30 meter	4 bar	2,5 liter	10 barl
40 meter	5 bar	2 liter	10 barl

No matter at what depth we look at the balloon, the product of pressure and volume always yields 10 barl.

Now you may wonder why you need to know this? Quick to explain: you need to know that so that you will not make a mistake one day that could cost you your life.

Let's construct a case that is not so outlandish. You snorkel and your dive partner dives with scuba tanks in your area. Now you dive down to him in apnea and give him the sign for "no air anymore / out of air situation"! So he gives you his regulator or the octopus regulator and you stay with him for a while, breathing out of the regulator. After a few breaths you want to get back to the surface and now Boyle and Mariotte become important. You breathed in out of the scuba in 10 meters of water depths. Thus you have in your lungs a pressure of 2 bar and an assumed volume of 5 liters of air. So twice the amount of air your lungs can handle at the surface. In this case namely 2 bar x 5 liters = 10 barl. As you emerge, without exhaling the 5 liters that are too much, your lungs will stretch and will most likely tear. Apart from the fact that nobody wishes that, the consequences can be quite lethal. Boyle Mariotte's law always works, whether you're diving from top to bottom, or from bottom to top. So in such a case, exhale as long as you can because it is better to reach the surface with a completely empty lung rather than an overstretched or torn lung.

4.4 The law of Gay Lussac

(French chemist and physicist 1778 to 1850)

The Law of Gay Lussac states that the pressure of an enclosed gas (in the scuba tank) changes with changing temperature if the volume stays steady (i.e. the volume of the scuba tank, for example 10 liters). That is, if the temperature rises, the pressure increases and the if temperature drops, the pressure also drops. When filling the tank gets very hot and the filling pressure is therefore about 220 bar. After cooling, the pressure is about 200 bar. This is physics and not a reason to sue the compressor operator for fraud. If the volume is constant, the pressure increase per degree Celsius with 1/273 of the pressure at zero degree Celsius. However, calculations are not expected until further education, so you can remain relaxed for the time being. Just take note that the pressure in your compressed air cylinder rises when heated and drops when cooled, that's enough.

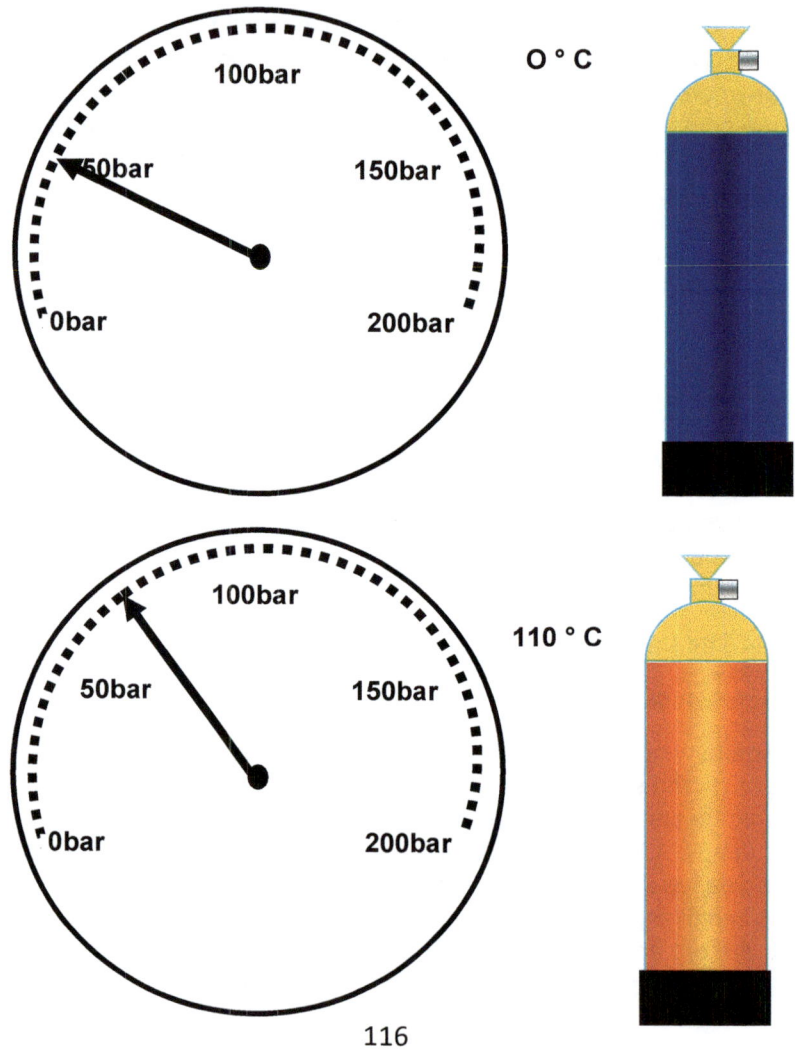

4.5 The law of Dalton (Dalton, John, English naturalist 1766 – 1844)

Maurice de Bevere, better known as Morris, helped me to understand the law of Dalton. As a comic fan, of course I am well-informed about the Daltons Joe, Jack, William and Averell and therefore knows that the convicts are always drawn like the organ pipes. Averell is the biggest and Joe is the smallest of the four. And together they make the Daltons. Sounds far-fetched, but it is not. Because I want to talk here about the composition of our most important breathing gas, and just as the air is a mixture of different gases, the Daltons are a mixture of different sized convicts. If Averell, the largest, represents the nitrogen **(N)** with 78% volume fraction, William is the oxygen **(O2)** at 21%, Jack the mix of **residual gases** at 0.96% is Joe the carbon dioxide **(CO2)** with 0, 04%! The whole thing is of course only for understanding, because Dalton has found that the individual gases in a gas mixture are always have a certain pressure and these pressures together give the total pressure of the gas mixture. This means that the Nitrogen, with 78 % volume fraction, is involved with 0.78 bar to the total pressure of 1 bar. These 0.78 bar is called the partial pressure of the Nitrogen at sea level. This means for Oxygen, with 21 % volume fraction, 0.21 bar partial pressure and for the residual gases with 1 % volume fraction, 0.01 bar partial pressure. A division of the residual gases in the actual partial pressures is not necessary for us scuba divers and would unnecessarily complicate the whole calculation. So now you know, when you hear Dalton, that these are the four crooks different in size and you can quickly transfer that to the different proportions of gases and their partial pressures. This is at least one of my donkey bridges (German for mnemonic), without which it is sometimes difficult to get along. I would like to show you now a sketch of the Daltons in conjunction with the partial pressures, but I'm afraid I will get terrible trouble due to copyright infringement. So please think of the Daltons yourself, because thinking is allowed.

P is for pressure again

P1 (N)   + P2 (O$_2$)   + P3 (Restgase) + P4 (CO$_2$)

= P total

0,78 bar   + 0,21 bar   + 0,006 bar   + 0,004 bar

= 1 bar

Averell   William   Jack   Joe

☺

It is the partial pressures that cause us the problems of diving. The pros avoid these problems by mixing the gases themselves and thus, for example in the case of nitrogen, reduce the depth intoxication or completely switch it off. But we beginners do not mix our breathing air for the time being, but take what nature has given us. Therefore, we have a lot to pay attention to. Many people who do not understand much about diving always talk about oxygen tanks and I always tell them that we dive and do not want to weld. Then I always explain to the ignorant that if we dive with pure oxygen, we would collapse at 4 meters according to recent findings. But, because Oxygen is a very reactive gas, the possibility is high that we fabricate an explosion during the filling process. Oxygen is a very aggressive gas and we have to pay attention to a lot of regulations if we want to fill the tanks with pure Oxygen. My tip, keep away from it and leave such things to the professionals.

Because most of us, including myself, are not diving doctors and therefore do not have their knowledge, we simply follow the recommendations of professionals in white coats.

If these doctors tell us that the oxygen we breathe is toxic (poisonous) from a partial pressure of 1.4 bar, then we believe it and avoid this partial pressure whenever possible.

So when is the oxygen in our breathing air under the partial pressure of 1.4 bar?

At 21% oxygen in our air, we have at the surface at one bar total pressure a partial pressure of 0.21 bar.

At a depth of 10 meters, we have a total pressure of 2 bar and this means twice the oxygen partial pressure, so 0.42 bar. Conclusion: Okay, it still works.

In 20 meters at a total pressure of 3 bar, we have 3 x 0.21 bar equal to 0.63 bar. Conclusion: still works.

In 30 meters we have a total pressure of 4 bar, so 4 x 0.21 bar equal to 0.84 bar. Conclusion: is still going.

In 40 meters we have a total pressure of 5 bar, so 5 x 0.21 equal to 1.05 bar. Conclusion: Everything is still good.

And here is now "closing time" for the ambitious scuba diver.

But when is the partial pressure of 1.4 bar reached?

We can now mathematically counteract this slowly or take a small formula to save time.

1.4 bar P O2 (oxygen partial pressure we want to have max.) divided by 0.21 bar (oxygen partial pressure prevailing at the surface) gives 6.66 bar ambient pressure.

We have 6.66 bar ambient pressure in 56.6 meters of water. Since we as recreational divers don't go so deep, we can ignore the oxygen as a "problem gas" completely.

Once again as a reminder. Scuba divers do not dive deeper than 40 meters. Don't forget it.

Now we could be happy and like Lucky Luke riding towards the sunset.

But there is still the nitrogen, which is present to 78% in our breathing air.

But there is always something. 😊

Of course, the physicians mentioned above have also given their thoughts on the subject of nitrogen and have discovered that nitrogen (N) acts narcotic from a partial pressure of 3.12 bar.

As mentioned above, this is different for each individual, but starting at 3.12 bar it is very likely that nitrogen will start to be toxic to you. To find out from which depth the gas now works toxic, we take again our little formula.

3.12 bar N divided by 0.78 bar is equal to 4 bar, so 30 meters of water.

And if we now take the maximum depth we are assigned? 40 meters equal to 5 bar.

5 bar by 0.78 bar is equal to 3.9 bar N partial pressure.

From the partial pressure of 3.9 bar N, our specialists say that the narcotic effect of nitrogen is so high that almost every scuba diver gets a deep intoxication. So it is quite good that we scuba divers dive never deeper than 40 meters anyway. It must be mentioned, however, that different people react differently to these partial pressures. While one feels a little bit strange at 20 meters, the other does not notice anything at 40 meters. ☺

So we prefer to stay in shallower climes to avoid nitrogen narcosis, because that's how the deep intoxication is called. Diving can and should give pleasure and no one has got anything out of it if we put ourselves unnecessarily in danger. If, despite everything, you want to go to 40 meters with a very experienced diver, watch out for your body and its responses to that depth. Become aware and if you feel unwell, give your partner the sign to reduce the depth or ascend until the surface. Do not bring yourself and your partner in danger, just to enter the 40 meters in your logbook. If you really need that depth, then go very slowly and by means of many dives to this depth, so that you get used to the nitrogen narcosis and become more resistant to it. Just so that we understand each other correctly, I refuse dives beyond 40 meters and go only to 40 meters, if there is a valid reason. Gold treasures and things like that. ☺

5. Diving practice

After having theorized a lot, apart from the introductory chapter, we now come to the practice. Of course, there are some things to consider here as well, and one would do well to follow these approved and established rules.

5.1 General rules

To avoid diving accidents the following should be known:

The diving equipment should

- correspond to the state of the art,

- be in a perfect condition,

- be operated easily.

In addition, the following principles apply:

- Never dive alone!

- Always pay attention of your dive partner, every second look

  applies to him or her.

- Get only so far away from your partner as you can

  dive in apnea.

- Dive, after the loss of your diving partner, after a short

  round view (also upwards), immediately to the surface.

- Never dive with malaise or if you have a cold.

- Never dive deeper than 40 meters.

- Never hold your breath (especially during a fast ascend).

- Always finish your dive with a minimum residual pressure of 50

  bar (safety reserve).

- The weakest in the dive group determines the tempo and the

  duration of the dive.

- The dive group goes together into the water and leaves

  it also together.

- Dive without a trace (do not touch or remove anything, perfect

  buoyancy)

At the beginning of each dive, a group leader is determined who already knows the diving area and has received the appropriate additional training. This group leader has at least the status Diver ** and the additional courses underwater orientation (compass) and group leadership completed, he should also be familiar with CPR and ideally he even has an oxygen rescue kit at hand. The recommended composition of the dive group can be found in the appendix.

But

Before it really starts and you dive with your dive partner, some things still have to be explained.

All members of the dive group must:

- know and how to use the contents of the emergency kit,

- be able to operate the oxygen rescue case,

- be able to make an emergency call (mobile, landline or radio),

- be able to provide first aid including CPR,

- be able to fill out a diving accident report (see form in

   the appendix).

Calculation basics of the dive!

- It will be calculated with the BMV (Breath minutes volume) of the

   diver with the largest BMV.

- If that is not known we expect a BMV from25 liters per Minute at

   the surface.

- There is always a safety decompression stop from 3 minutes

   onto 5 Meters.

- The calculations are always according to the current

   regulations.

 - Only No-stop time dives are performed.

After these prerequisites are all met, there is a briefing, which means a report what we want to do during the following dive. The Americans always say: Plan your dive and dive your plan! And by that they mean that what they have planned for this dive they have to follow exactly.

If you suddenly find the gold treasure during your planned dive, sorry I still hope to find one and cannot get it out of my head either, leave it to the left or to the right. Inhumane, I know, but this treasure could, with a little bit of bad luck, cost you your life. You probably dive spontaneously too deep and too long to grab the treasure and then pay attention neither to your air supply nor to any decompression stops to be observed. Apart from a dive partner who thinks the same and who wants to have the gold perhaps for himself alone. Of course, as mentioned above, this is nonsense, but perhaps you will suddenly find an unknown and recently sunken ship or a cave that is new to you. Then the adventurer in the diver gets the upper hand if that is not counteracted. In such a case, ascend to the surface and consult with your partner how you want to proceed. You then have to evaluate all aspects and plan and calculate a completely new dive. It will take time, but your life is worth more than anything you hope to find in the wreck or cave.

Plan your dive and dive your plan!

5.2 The Briefing (discussion before the dive)

What belongs in such a briefing?

- Purpose of the dive (Loose relaxation dive or exercises?)

- Dive depth and dive time

- Who is the group leader

- Group size depending on the view, within larger groups

  form teams of two

- Dangers under water? Current, animals, ships ….

- Rescue chain! Where and under what phone number can the

  Emergency call be made?

- Oxygen case and emergency kit are in which place

  and are they ready?

- Speak about the UW signs

- Clarify and explain environmental conditions (wind, ice, stronger

  rain, fog etc.)

- Clarify positions under water (group leader in front, a good

  diver with experience at the end of the group)

- Behavior in case of partner loss (always stay together)

  what have we to do to prevent a partner loss

Now it goes into the water (almost).

Now we have everything observed and stand, fully equipped, on the car or already on the shore. Hint, run the partner check, which has to come now, on the car. Often you forget a small thing, for example the lead belt and then have to go all the way back to the car to fetch it. Meanwhile, colleagues probably start to freeze or sweat and are already annoyed before it even starts. If you dive from the boat, you have it more easy there; but just if you have not forgotten anything in the car.

But, contrary to expectations, nobody has forgotten something and now follows the partner check or buddy check.

5.3 The partner check or buddy check!

Why?

If you have to save your partner, which will hopefully never happen, you need to know how and if the partner's equipment works. Since there are different manufacturers, there are also different systems and it is important that you are able to open your partner's lead belt buckle or press the correct inflator button, even in the darkest water. On the shore and just before the dive, look closely at your partner's equipment and have them explain it to you if you are unsure. Also check the functions of each piece of the equipment. When you realize underwater that your partner has forgotten to connect low-pressure hose of the inflator can this put you in distress if he sinks or you cannot bring him to the surface.

At the partner check, first look at the tank and check that the valve is completely open. We remember that the valve is turned up to the stop and then turned back about a quarter turn, in order to protect the seals of the spindle on the one hand and make it easier to check the opening state of the valve on the other hand. There are very strong people who turn the valve when opening so strong to the left stop, that when checking we can't be sure whether the valve is now open or closed, because you cannot turn it. Therefore, always a quarter turn back and then it is easy to see the opening state of the valve Then look at the pressure gauge to check the pressure of the tank. It should be at the beginning of the dive 200 bar or slightly higher. Or at 300 bar devices that are rather uncommon with us recreational divers, at about 300 bar. While looking at the pressure gauge, carefully and briefly actuate the air knob of the regulator. Please check both second stages, paying attention to the pointer of the finimeter. Also make sure that the escaping air does not flow into anyone's face. If the pointer remains at 200 bar in this test, everything is okay, if it falls towards 0 bar, the valve is either closed or defective (the measuring bore of the pressure gauge may also be clogged, but that is rare). Then check the BCD (Jacket). Press the inflator and let so much air into the BCD until the relief valve audibly blows off. As a result, you have the function of this safety device also checked. One or the other dive partner will complain because you are wasting the precious air and he lose a minute underwater. Put this remark in the folder "Safety first". If your partner during the dive realizes that the safety valve is out of order and the bladder bursts he will understand why you made this test. But then it is too late. Fortunately, this hardly ever happens. Check all the air outlet options of the jacket. As already mentioned many jackets have an integrated air outlet in the pleated hose of the jacket. Then you can grab the whole hose on the inflator unit and vent the jacket by pulling on the pleated hose. A diving partner of mine had once made a self-service on his jacket and completely disassembled, cleaned and reassembled. Such services, even with the regulator, will be made again and again from technically interested divers. My tip: Leave such service activities to the professionals. To come back to my colleague, it should be mentioned that we jumped from a bridge into the Baltic Sea, filled our jackets and then got ready for the dive. After the okay sign, I vented my jacket slowly and carefully while my colleague pulled on the pleated tube. The pleated hose is usually attached to the jacket by means of a gas-tight fitting and this fitting requires the use of special tools to ensure the correct torque, i.e. the strength of the screw connection. If, like my colleague, you are not in possession of this special tool, you will simply assembling the hose like an amateur. The receipt for his botch he got promptly served, because the entire pleated hose unit broke up on the jacket and the jacket took just under 2 seconds to empty completely. The only stupid thing was that the colleague had not yet had his regulator in his mouth and now sailed relatively quickly to the seabed. Since he is an accomplished diver, then especially this divers tinker with their equipment, this did not kill him and he could, shortly after hitting the ground in almost 10 meters water depth, put the second stage in his mouth and breathe. If a beginner or an untrained diver comes into such a situation, it is not always guaranteed that he will keep a cool mind. In that case, immediate throwing off of the lead belt would have been an appropriate response.

Conclusion: Leave all screw driving on your equipment to the professionals, because they have not only the right tools, but also visited the appropriate training courses of the manufacturers.

Then check if your partner has all the necessary equipment:

- Computer and/or Decompression table with watch and depth

   gauge

- divers mask

- fins

- lead belt and/or lead pockets in the jacket

- divers knife or scissors

- gloves

- snorkel

- compass (makes only sense if dealing with it is known)

- divers flag (Alpha)

- possibly wetnotes with pencil

- possibly UW camera

- possibly divers torch

- possibly reel (a Roll with a thin rope (20 to 50 Meter)

- possibly safety or decompression buoy

And then, of course, everything that creeps in over the years. For example, a magnifying glass to read the dive computer or compass even in advanced age. Of course, a diving mask with optical lenses is better. There are even progressive lenses for the diving mask.

Diver in full (dry) gear.

Now you can finally go down. Elegant and without churning up the water with the fins. Remember, it will not do any good if you flog the surface of the water or even the air above it with your fins. The thrust that should bring you down only starts when the fin leaves are completely submerged. In addition, it looks to the outsider, as if there is a "beginner" trying to dive. And we want to avoid that of course.

When diving, always make sure (at least every 5 to 10 seconds, depending on the visibility under water), whether your dive partner is with you. If not, the dive will be canceled and you will return to the surface to meet your dive partner there.

At a pre-determined depth, make a short stop to make sure your and your partner's equipment is working properly and is not blowing off (bubble check). And now you can finally start. Please be aware that as a Diver * or Open Water Diver, you will always dive together with experienced divers who lead the group or just you. From these divers you can learn a lot and become more sure from dive to dive and approach your next dive course to Advanced Open Water Diver or Diver **.

5.4 Environmental friendly behavior

Diving is, in addition to the technology we need for it, a natural sport. At the latest, you know why it is a sport, if you have towed all your equipment 200 meters over the beach to go diving at this very special dive site. For such hardships, there are endless examples, so you must always be healthy and fit if you want to go diving.

For example, you may not mow through the reed belt like a bulldozer if you want to cut the 200 meters to the dive site. In the reeds birds could breed or hide animals, which are probably be disturbed by you unnecessarily.

What else needs to be avoided?

- Use only paved roads and designated Parking lots, if you arrive

  by car.

- Avoid the noise pollution of local residents and the

  wildlife (no compressor operation on site).

- Leave the dive site the way you want to found it.

- Take your trash back with you. But it is allowed too

  to remove trash if it was there before.

- Leave the water as you would like to find it

(Trusting that you are not a messie).

- Take advantage of existing entry-level opportunities, such as bathing jetties or the beach.
- Pay attention to spawning and breeding places.
- If you arrive by boat, there are special things to be observed. Take for example anchor buoys and do not throw the anchor carelessly into the water.
- Tare well to avoid whirling up sediment or damaging corals.
- Attach your equipment to your body so that it does not damage anything. For example, if you dive over the reef roof (eg, pressure gauge or the second stage).
- Do not dive through the plant belts.
- Do not touch anything.
- Do not hunt fishes. Harpooning is strictly banned in Germany for example and the use of it will be punished.
- Do not collect shells, snails or similar. You have already enough dust catcher in the domestic shelf.
- Engage in water cleaning actions, but do not take out everything that looks like garbage. First, have a look inside and see if there is not a fish or a crab living there. This little animals love empty tanks or cans.
- Adjust the number of divers and dives to the diving site.
- Do not dive to the spawning times of the fish in the lake.

- Take special care when diving in winter.

 Don't disturb the fishes, may be they could die

 because they are set for winter hibernation.

5.5 The dive calculation

And now we come to the discipline that most prefer to avoid, namely the

Calculation of dives.

But sometimes it cannot be avoided and is not as complicated as you might think.

By far the greater part of your dives in the future, probably will take place without any calculation. A classic dive that requires no calculation is a dive in your "home waters"! You know your maximum depth, your average dive time, and at the end of the dive, you will make your safety stop of 3 minutes at 5 meters to pave the way for one or the other micro-bubble that might have crept in. Pay attention to your dive computer or the depth gauge, find out in advance about the no-stop time in your maximum depth and have a look at your pressure gauge. By this already the most important aspects are ticked off.

Also make sure that you stay in no-stop time and that you always have enough air for the return and the ascent. In such a "house dive" the maximum depth is usually at most 15 meters and there you have at least 72 minutes no-stop time including the descent time. If you are in a wet suit, 72 minutes are a long time, depending on the water temperature. Especially as the water temperature decreases with increasing depth, up to about 4 degrees Celsius. Water has a so-called density anomaly, so it is not normal in terms of density with respect to temperature. In practice, this means that the water at temperatures above and below 4 degrees Celsius reduces its density and thus "floats"!

Therefore, the temperature at the bottom of a lake, of course, depending on currents and turbulences, always is at 4 degrees Celsius, colder water and warmer water goes up.

If you dive with professionals, anyway the guide or instructor takes the lead and thus also a possible dive calculation. On the basis of the respective displays of the pressure gauge, the dive is then carried out under constant observation of the different filling conditions of the diving devices of the group. Again, the weakest determines the duration of the dive. If the weakest person reaches the 50 bar after only a short time, he usually gets the octopus of the group leader with whom he can then continue the dive, so as not to unnecessarily shorten the other diver's dive. However, that depends on the respective group leader.

To calculate a dive, we need, among other things, the amount of air that such a person needs within a minute at the surface (BMV). Of course, this amount depends on some factors above or under water, and can never be determined exactly.

If we lie down on the couch and watch a "Cornwall movie", the respiratory rate of some of us goes back very much and then often leading to a deep and refreshing sleep. In such a case we inhale about 0.5 liters per breath. This amount of air that we inhale and exhale per breath is referred to as tidal volume, in this case 0.5 liters.

If you change the channel to, for example, "Shades of Gray", the tidal volume might increase to over 0.8 liters. If you have an easy training on the ergometer, the tidal volume can easily increase to 3 liters and more. In addition, the respiratory rate, which is at rest at 12 to 15 breaths per minute, can increase, under heavy load, up to 60 breaths per minute and more. You have probably experienced this even while jogging or cycling.

Now these are not defined values, they are individually different, so we have to take an average value. The doctors have set that to 25 liters per minute. So we consume 25 liters of respiratory air per minute, at the sea surface, abbreviated to BMV (breathing minute volume). This is a relatively safe value as most people are below it.

So, 25 liters of BMV, at sea level, is the value we use for our calculation. Please remember!

According to the law of Boyle Mariotte, we also have to consider the respective ambient pressure, because starting from 25 liters of BMV per minute at the sea surface, we need at 10 meters water depth, with twice the ambient pressure, also twice the amount of BMV. So 50 liters BMV to 10 meters water depth. At 20 meters, that would be 75 liters per minute, 30 meters 100 liters and 40 meters 125 liters. We can already see that we need more and more air with increasing water depth. That is one reason why, in the case of "larger" diving events, we must first calculate how much air we need. Fortunately, such calculations are pure multiplications, so pressure multiplicated with the volume, and that's all. Incidentally, pressure multiplicated with the volume also applies to our diving tanks. So if we have a 10 liter standard tank and fill it with a pressure of 200 bar we have 10 liters times 200 bar and this equates to 2000 barl (Barliter).

Here are some simple calculations of volume content to get used to:

Tank volume	x	Filling pressure	=	Content in barl
10 liter		200 bar		2000 barl
12 liter		200 bar		2400 barl
15 liter		220 bar		3300 barl
10 liter		180 bar		1800 barl
20 liter		200 bar		4000 barl

And so on and so on, quite simply. Volume times pressure equal to air content in liters or barliters (barl).

Let us now turn to our first calculation:

We want to dive 10 meters deep and stay there for 20 minutes, including the dive time, to photograph a sea turtle.

For safety reasons, we calculate the total bottom time, i.e. the time we need from "head under water" until the beginning of the ascent, with the maximum possible ambient pressure during this dive. At a depth of 10 meters there is a pressure of 2 bar and as we stick to our diving plan (Plan your dive and dive your plan) this is also the maximum possible pressure that awaits us. The decompression table gives a no-decompression time (no-stop time) of 140 minutes for 12 meters and since we only stay down for 20 minutes, we are absolutely sure to get no decompression sickness. So now we only have the variable time we need for the ascent.

Of course, there are also specifications and they say:

Water depth	Ascent rate
40 – 20 Meter	18 Meter / Minute
20 – 10 Meter	10 Meter / Minute
10 – 0 Meter	8 Meter / Minute

The greater the depth we have been in, the higher the ambient pressure we have been exposed to, and thus the "saturation" with nitrogen has been higher. So we have to ascent slowly in order to be able to exhale the excess nitrogen. Since we have the greatest pressure difference from 0 to 10 meters or vice versa, namely a doubling on the way down and a halving on the way up, we have to make for safety reasons a safety decompression stop from 3 minutes to 5 meters. The diving doctors say that we should be able to maintain a maximum ascent rate of 8 meters per minute. However, to avoid complicated comma numbers in the calculation, we simply round to 5 meters per minute, which is a step in the "healthier direction". If you want, you can of course use the calculator and continue to calculate with 8 meters, which is quite permissible and since we do not always dive in 10 meter steps, are not always avoidable comma numbers anyway.

Calculation:

Bottom time: 20 minutes

Depth: 10 meter

Ascent time: 2 minutes (with 5 meters per minute)

Dekostopp: 3 minutes at 5 meters

BMV: 25 liter per minute

Now we have all the numbers we need to figure out how much air we need for this dive.

So now we have to multiply the bottom time with the ambient pressure and the BMV to get the amount of air we need for this dive, until the beginning of the ascent.

Bottom time in minutes x max. ambient pressure in bar x Breathing minute volume (BMV)

20 minutes x 2 bar x 25 liter / minute = 1000 barl

The ascent must be added now:

Ascent time to the surface x max. Ambient pressure x breathing minute volume (BMV)

2 minutes x 2 bar x 25 liter / minute = 100 barl

And now the safety decompression stop:

3 minutes x 1,5 bar (pressure at 5 meters water depth) x 25 liter / minute = 112,5 barl

So we need for this dive:

1000 barl for the bottom time

100 barl for the ascent

112,5 barl for the safety stop

Total amount of air: <u>1212,5 barl</u>

Let's assume that we dive with our standard tank, the 10 liter unit, we get the following result:

The tank is filled with 200 bar and thus contains 2000 barl. Now we have to subtract the 50 bar reserve, because we **never** attack them. So:

50 bar x 10 liter = 500 barl

The 500 barl we subtract, as a reserve, now from the 2000 barl and receive 1500 barl, which we may consume.

For our above calculated dive we need 1212,5 barl and have 1500 barl available.

For us, this means that we can perform this dive safely with the standard tank of 10 liters, which is filled with 200 bar. At least as far as the amount of air is concerned, if we stick to our plan. In addition to the 500 barl reserve we still have 287.5 barl left over.

This calculation we have explained in detail, the following calculations are somewhat "sober" and more "formulaic" carried out. But this is always the same thing, it just looks a little more professional. ☺

The bottom time is marked by: $\downarrow$

The ascent time is marked by: $\uparrow$

The deco stop is marked by: $\longrightarrow$

Dive: 20 m max. depth (3 bar)

Bottom time: 18 minutes

BMV: 25 liter / minute

Safety stop: 3 minutes / 5 meters

How big must our tank be?

$\downarrow$ 18 minutes x 25 liter/min. x 3 bar = **1350 barl**

$\uparrow$ 4 minutes x 25 liter/min. x 3 bar = **300 barl**

$\longrightarrow$ 3 minutes x 25 liter/min. x 1,5 bar = **112,5 barl**

Total amount: **1762,5 barl**

The reserve is, at 200 bar filling pressure, 50 bar or 25% of the filling pressure.

We need 1762.5 barl for this dive and this represents 75% of the required volume.

Now to get the 100% of the required volume, namely the 75% consumption plus 25% reserve, we divide the 1762.5 barl by 75 and then multiply that value by 100 and we have the 100% we need.

1762,5 barl : 75 = 23,5 barl

23,5 barl x 100 = 2350 barl

In order to get the volume of the required diving tank, we have to divide this amount of air by 200 (the filling pressure).

2350 barl: 200 bar = 11,75 Liter

So we need, at least, a diving tank with the volume of 11.75 liters at 200 bar filling pressure.

Now it's a bit of a hassle for the industry to make a specific tank for each of our newly calculated dives, so we'll take the next-standard volume, 12 liters, or whoever appreciates the more even weight distribution and lower center of gravity of a double-tank, perhaps a double 7. Both are suitable and of course everything in volume above it. But think about your back.☺

5.6 The use of the decompression table

The Deco 2000 by Dr. med. Max Hahn is available in two variants.

The first table (blue) is valid for the range 0 - 700m above normal zero (above sea level).

The second table (green) is valid for the range of 701 - 1500m (above sea level).

We first look at the blue decompression table.

At the front of the decompression table you'll find in the left column of the table the depth data printed in bold type. Below this is the respective no-stop time.

The **no-stop time** is the maximum allowable time from leaving the water surface until beginning of ascent without having to comply with a decompression stop.

The **bottom time** is the actual or planned time from leaving the water surface (head under water) until the beginning of the ascent.

In the column next to the depth indication with the no-stop time are a few bottom times listed.

Always **read to the safe side** when determining a time or a depth.

The safe side is always the one where the risk of a decompression accident is the smallest.

Right next to it are times, in minutes, for a required Deko stop in the respective depth column to find. If no deco stops are required, the field is white deposited. If Deco stops are required, the field is blue (green in the table for altitude dives/ mountain lakes) deposited.

The letters to the right of this column indicate the so-called Repetition group. You need this information to determinate the fictitious time surcharge, depending of the surface pause. You find the time surcharge on the backside of the decompression table and you have to add this time surcharge to the dive time of your second dive because the second dive is a so-called repetitive dive.

Important note:

In cold conditions or short strong effort you have to use the next higher time step.

If the dive has been with a long hard effort, 50% is added to the bottom time.

Example:

We have made the first dive at the sea in a water depth of 31 m with a bottom time of 16 min. After a surface break of 2 h 45 min is a second dive planned in a water depth of 20 m and with a bottom time of 13 min.

We have made the first dive at the sea in a water depth of 31 m with a bottom time of 16 min. So we have to use the next larger depth of 33 m in the table.

In these depth boxes, we now use the next larger bottom time, namely 18 min.
Now the decompression break of 5 min in 3m water depth can be read on the right.
The repetition group is E.
This repeating group is now needed as a second dive is to be performed on that day.
After a surface break of 2 h 45 min, we choose for the second dive a depth of 20 m and a bottom time of 13 min.
Since our body has stored a certain amount of residual nitrogen after the first dive, it is necessary that at the bottom time of the next dive, a time supplement is determined and added.
We can do this with the previously determined repetition group E from the table.

In this case, due to the surface pause of 2 h 45min between 2:30 and 3:00 the relevant column will be determined.
Since the depth of the second dive should be 20 m, the depth of the repetitive dive at 18 m is now used in the table.
The safe side in this case is the smaller depth because the time surcharge is higher.
The calculated time surcharge of 19 min is added to the planned bottom time of 13 min.
With this total bottom time of 32 min, the next larger bottom time of 36 min is read in the table in the box for 21 m.
Now a decompression break from 2 min at 3 m can be read on the right. The repetition group is now F.

If we would read the depth of the repetition dive at 21 m to determine the time surcharge, we would have a lower time surcharge of 16 min.

Adding this time surcharge to the planned basic time of 13 minutes, we get a total base time of only 29 minutes.

Readed in the depth box for 21 m, this incorrectly determined value for the bottom time would still be in the no-stop time.

The safe side for determining the time surcharge is always the one with the higher time surcharge.

If the surface pause is exactly 2 h 30 min, you have to read following our example (repetitive group E) in the column between 2:00 and 2:30 because the time surcharges are higher in the column below.

If the depth of the planned dive falls between two depths of the table (depth of repetitive dive), the shallower depth is taken because the time surcharge there is larger again.

With the larger time surcharge, the amount of residual nitrogen remaining in the body after the first dive is taken into account.

With a smaller time surcharge, a smaller residual amount of nitrogen remaining in the body would be fooled.

For the decompression of the second dive can have fatal consequences!

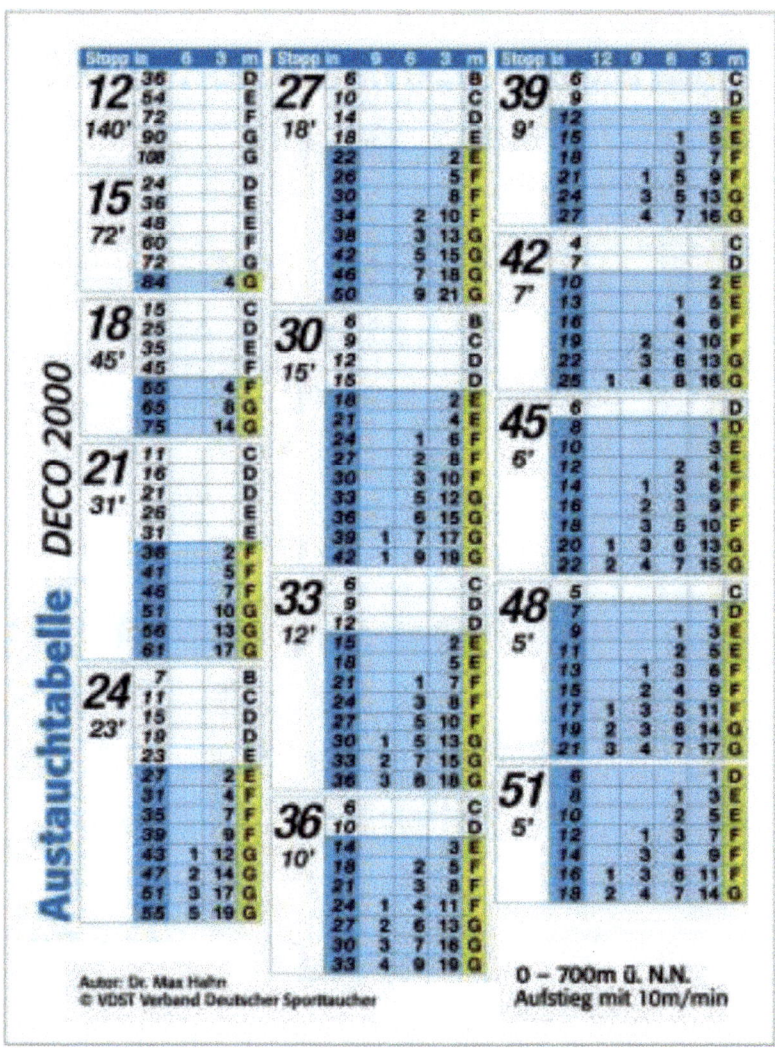

Autor: Dr. Max Hahn

©VDST Verband Deutscher Sporttaucher

To be acquired via the VDST-Shop

143

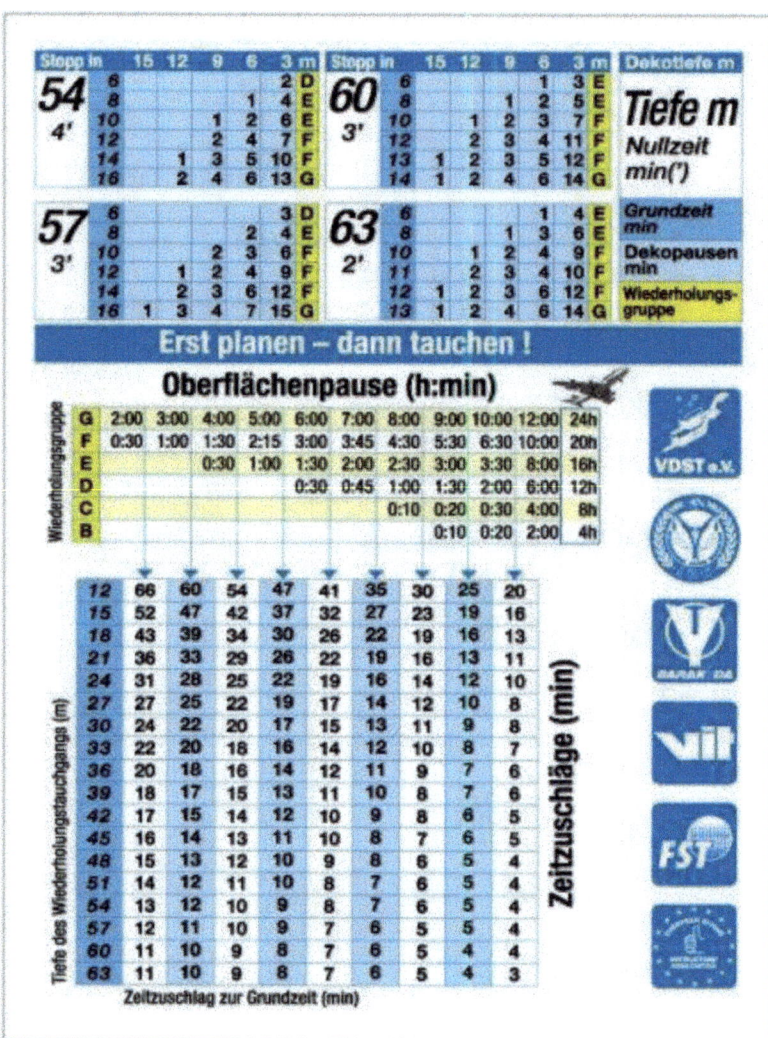

Autor: Dr. Max Hahn

©VDST Verband Deutscher Sporttaucher

To be acquired via the VDST-Shop

Notes on dive calculations with the Deko 2000

For dive calculations, the descent is calculated at a descent rate of 30 m / min and the air consumption at the highest dive depth is calculated.
During the ascent we calculate with a ascent rate, depending on the max. depth, from 18m to 8m / min and the air consumption also is calculated onto the largest depth.
The air consumption of the decompression stages is calculated according to the respective depth.

5.7 Notes for mountain lake diving / altitude diving

If we move from sea level to higher mountain regions, the ambient pressure drops (see also page 12).
At a mountain lake in, for example, 3500m altitude, we only have an ambient pressure of about 0.65bar.
A change in altitude has a negative effect on the personal efficiency due to the decreased oxygen pressure. The body needs some time to get used to the changed environmental conditions. If we were permanently at sea level, we still have some residual nitrogen due to the reduced ambient pressure in the blood. For us, the first dive would be a repetitive dive. The risk of a decompression accident increases significantly. The body also needs a certain amount of time to breathe off this amount of residual nitrogen. For these two reasons we should acclimatize for at least one day.
Due to the altered pressure conditions above and below water, there is a change in nitrogen saturation or - desaturation.
Accordingly, other decompression tables apply.
With increasing mountain altitude, the ambient pressure decreases after the ascent.
This means that as the altitude of the mountain increases, the nitrogen partial pressure increases in the last few meters of going up. As a result, the ascent times are prolonged, in contrast to the ascent times at sea level, and the decompression stages must be done at shallower depths to avoid decompression sickness.

Likewise, the no-stop times are shortened.
There are corresponding correction calculations for the use of the marine level tables or for altitude diving tables.

5.8 Hints for diving after or before flying

The cabin interior air is kept dry for technical reasons, which leads to a slow but steady dehydration, especially on long-haul flights. The risk of a decompression accident with a dive performed on the day of arrival may thereby be increased.
The reduced cabin pressure also affects the mucous membranes in the sinuses, resulting in pressure equalization problems with a dive performed on the day of arrival.
The jet lag that occurs especially on long-haul flights through several time zones additionally upsets our sense of time and our sleep-wake rhythm.
This can lead to insomnia, fatigue, dizziness, mood swings, loss of appetite, and diminished performance in physical, manual, and cognitive (mental) demands.

For these reasons, IDA recommends that we acclimatize for at least one day and drink a lot (water, juices or tea).

If additional alcohol is consumed during the flight, experience has shown this often happens, a dive on the day of arrival is in any case forbidden.

After each dive there is a barely avoidable residual saturation in the body. This means that not every nitrogen could be completely exhaled because this process takes time. This fact is not bad at all, since the calculations of dive times using decompression tables take this into account. However, when we board a plane to fly home or to the next dive destination, we must take into account that the pressure inside the cabin of the aircraft is reduced to about 0.7 bar.
This reduction in ambient pressure can now lead to a decompression sickness, since we are not completely desaturated. Therefore it is strongly recommended

to avoid any flight at least 24 hours after diving. My tip, wait 48 hours with your next flight, because then your "diving clothes" are completely dried, (except for the boots that never dry :-) and your suitcase smells not so bad unpacking it.

5.9 Emergency card

See the both following pages

Emergency card for divers / diving accidents

To be noted by the doctor.

The holder of this card is a diver.

If there is evidence of decompression sickness (often discrete neurological symptoms such as paresthesia, tingling, numbness and paralysis, other nonspecific symptoms are possible), treatment in a hyperbaric chamber is essential, and may even be life-saving.

Initial treatment: Give Oxygen 100 % (Pay attention to pre-existing conditions) and a lot of fluid (water).

Please have the accident victim immediately taken to a hospital or a pressure chamber treatment center where diving accidents can be treated.

Maximum altitude for helicopter transport 300 meter.

First aid

Performed first aid measures (mark with a cross):

O Artificial respiration   Duration:_____

O Cardiopulmonary resuscitation (CPR)   Duration:_____

O Oxygen administration   Duration:_____

Administration of medication:

_____

Pulse:_____

Respiratory rate:_____

Blood pressure:_____

Previous dive:_____ Depth:_____ Surface pause:_____

Repetitive group:_____

Date of the accident dive:_____ Start:_____ End:_____

Max. depth:_____ Duration of the dive:_____

Used gas mixture/Breathing gas:_____

Decompression time and depth:_____

Dive site:_____ sea level or altitude dive:_____

Special feature:_____

148

Personal data of the diver

Name:_____ First name:_____

Born:_____

Street:_____ Zip code:_____

City:_____ Country:_____

Telephone:_____ mobile:_____

Who should be notified:_____ Telephone:_____

Medical history:_____

Illness:_____

Will medications be taken:_____ Which drugs:_____

Dive data

Dives total:_____ Training condition:_____

Training level:_____ Diving medical examination valid:_____

Name and address of the diving partner:_____

_____

Additional information

Date and name of the doctor:_____

Attached documents or equipment:_____

O Logbook   O dive computer   O gas sample   O tank   O other

Helplines

DAN International Emergencies +39-06-42118685

aquamed emergency hotline: +49-(0) 70034835463

We wish a lot of wonderful dives and hope that you never need this document. But, for safety reasons, fill out this form with everything you know and take it always with you when you dive.

149

6.0 Diving with Nitrox

If we take it exactly, we always use Nitrox, namely Nitrox 21. Since the number after the word Nitrox indicates the percentage of oxygen in the gas mixture. Nitrox is an artificial word made up of the two main gases that are used.

Nitrogen and **Ox**ygen

Abroad, one usually uses the term EAN or EANx, which stands for Enriched Air Nitrox.

Why should we, if possible, dive with Nitrox?

Diving with Nitrox has enjoyed increasing popularity for over 20 years and is one of the most booked courses worldwide. By using Nitrox as a breathing gas you can extend your dives or you can dive safer within the same dive time as with normal air with regard to nitrogen saturation. Even with several dives a day, so-called repetitive dives, there is a positive effect on health when diving with Nitrox. This effect is due to the fact that when we dive with nitrox, we take in less nitrogen. The normal breathing air with which we usually dive contains about 78% nitrogen and 21% oxygen. Both gases behave differently, depending on the ambient pressure, and thus their effect on the human body changes, depending on the pressure we are exposed to. The residual gases (1%) (noble gases, carbon dioxide, water vapor, etc.) are negligible.

The lower the nitrogen partial pressure, i.e. the proportion of nitrogen in the total gas mixture, the less is the risk of decompression sickness and the danger of a depth intoxication. In which, according to the latest research, the previously assumed reduced risk of getting a depth intoxication, seems to be like diving with air. Since oxygen, inhaled under increased pressure, has a narcotic effect too and thus differs only slightly from the nitrogen narcosis (depth intoxication). But this effect is currently only of a theoretical nature, because there are no empirical studies yet.

On the other hand, however, the proportion of oxygen in our gas mixture determines the maximum depth we are allowed to go to. The higher the oxygen content, the lower the allowed depth with the corresponding mixture. If you have internalized this theory lesson and successfully completed the course Nitrox with your instructor, you may dive with a maximum oxygen content of 40% in the mixture used.

If you then enjoy diving with different gases, you can visit many different courses offered by our IDA Instructors.

IDA Nitrox Advanced

Gas Blender (mix gases by yourself)

SCR (Semi-closed Rebreather)

Trimix* and ** (Nitrogen, Helium and Oxygen)

Nitrox-Basic-Instructor

Nitrox-Instructor

Nitrox-Instructor Examiner

Trimix-Instructor

Trimix-Instructor Examiner

But let's start very slowly.

When we start to dive with a different gas than normal breathing air, new terms come to mind that are due to the different compositions of Nitrox.

On this page we summarized and explained these.

EAN   Enriched Air Nitrox   = with oxygen enriched air

EANx Enriched Air Nitrox   = with oxygen enriched air

MOD   Maximum Operating Depth   = Maximum depth of dive

MOP   Maximum Operating Pressure   = Maximum ambient pressure at the chosen depth

EAD   Equivalent Air Depth = Equivalent depth when diving with air

EAP   Equivalent Air Pressure   = Equivalent pressure when diving with air

Best Mix   =   Optimum mix for this depth and dive time

OTU   Oxygen Tolerance Unit   = Tolerated oxygen units

CNS   Central Nervous System   = Central Nervous System :-)

CNS O_2%   =   Relative toxicity of O2 for the CNS

NOAA National Oceanic and Atmospheric Administration (USA)

Here are some examples of common nitrox compositions:

Nitrox 32 = 32% O_2 + 68% N_2 = **EAN 32**

Nitrox 36 = 36% O_2 + 64% N_2 = **EAN 36**

Nitrox 40 = 40% O_2 + 60% N_2 = **EAN 40**

IDA recommends a maximum oxygen partial pressure (ppO2) of 1.4 bar (pp stands for partial pressure)

Therefore, the oxygen content in the gas mixture automatically results in the maximum diving depth.

32 % is equal to 0,32 bar ppO_2 at the surface.

36 % is equal to 0,36 bar ppO_2 at the surface.

40 % is equal to 0,40 bar ppO_2 at the surface.

Based on a maximum oxygen partial pressure (gas partial pressure) of 1.4 bar, we come to the following water depths. We divide the 1.4 bar ppO2 by the oxygen partial pressure at the water surface and then receive the max. partial pressure of oxygen and can deduce the maximum depth of it.

Nitrox 32 (NOAA Nitrox 1) = 4,38 bar corresponds to 33,8 meter

Nitrox 36 (NOAA Nitrox 2) = 3,9 bar corresponds to 29 meter

Nitrox 40 = 3,5 bar corresponds to 25 meter

Nitrox 50 (Safe air) = 2,8 bar corresponds to 18 meter

 Attention, not always stands the oxygen content of the gas mixture at the first place. It is always necessary to analyze the mixture before use.

 In addition, other organizations have others standard gas mixtures.

So you have to check the oxygen content of the used mixture before <u>each</u> dive! Make sure your scuba tank is not swapped after oxygen analysis.

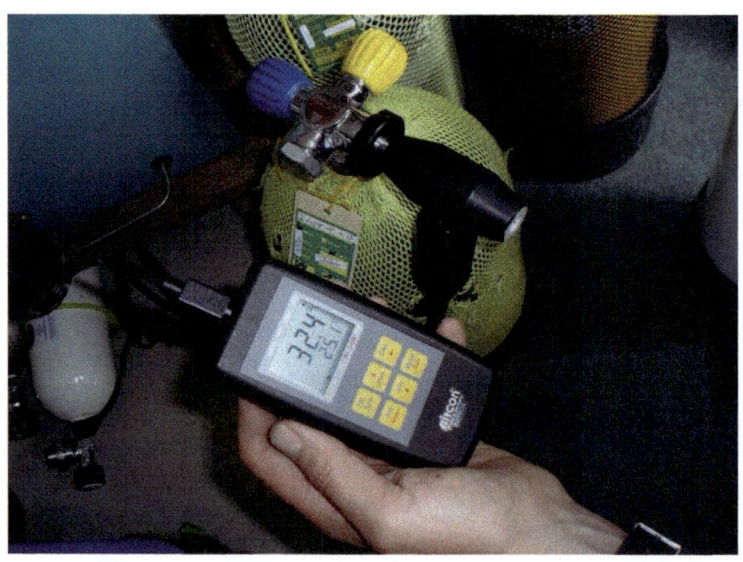

The previous analysis shows an oxygen content of 32.4%!

So Nitrox 32!

The gas mixture should always be mixed as precisely as possible and the difference to the calculated gas, should always be as low as possible, but at any rate below 1%, larger differences can lead to accidents or even death. Get yourself introduced to the analyzer if you do not have an own with whom you have gained experience. Always check the oxygen content of your breathing air yourself!

What is oxygen?

Oxygen (O_2)

- is a colorless and odorless element

- is a molecule in double bond

- boiling point: -183° C

- density: 1,429 Kg/m³

- is not flammable in pure form

- is necessary for the combustion process

- acts as an oxidizer

- acts as a fire accelerator with increasing

  concentration

What is nitrogen?

Nitrogen (N_2)

- is a colorless and odorless element

- is a molecule in double bond

- boiling point: -194,6° C

- density: 1,25 Kg/m^3

- makes as "inert gas" hardly any biochemical

  connections

What is carbon dioxide?

Carbon dioxide (CO_2)

- is a compound of 1 atom C and 2 atoms O_2

- is colorless and odorless

- is easily soluble in liquids (e. g. in mineral water)

- boiling point: -78,5° C

- density: 1,977 Kg/m^3

Gases and their application limits!

Oxygen

Minimal ppO_2 = 0,16 bar

Maximum ppO_2 = 1,4 bar

Nitrogen

At approx. 3.2 bar ppN2, an increased anesthetic symptom (depth intoxication) can be expected.

Carbon dioxide

Maximum ppCO2 0.05 bar in the arterial blood (from 0.06 bar ppCO2 hypercapnia can be expected and CO2 anesthesia can occur)

The partial pressures in the water depth can be easily calculated by multiplying the partial pressure of the individual gas at the water surface, with the ambient pressure in the depth.

Example

32 % oxygen is equal to a partial pressure (ppO$_2$) of 0,32 bar

In 20 meters of water, there is an ambient pressure of 3.0 bar.

So we now multiply the ambient pressure with the partial pressure and thus come to the partial pressure, which prevails at this specific depth.

0,32 bar ppO$_2$ x 3,0 bar = 0.96 bar ppO$_2$

Our oxygen partial pressure at a water depth of 20 meters is therefore 0.96 bar. So completely uncritical.

We know that we are allowed to have a maximum oxygen partial gas pressure of 1.4 bar. So we can divide 1.4 bar by 0.32 bar to come to the maximum allowable ambient pressure.

1.4 bar divided by 0.32 bar gives 4.375 bar

This 4.375 bar is the maximum permissible ambient pressure with an oxygen content of 32%.

We have 4.375 bar ambient pressure in a water depth of 33.75 meters. (We have to subtract the 1.0 bar air pressure at the surface, i.e. 3.375 bar water pressure)

This results in a maximum permitted depth of 33.75 meters with an oxygen content of 32%!

This calculation can be used for any gas mixture.

If you want, you can also use the following formula.

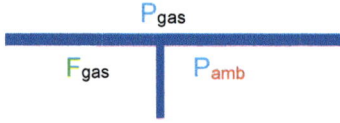

P_{Gas} stands for the partial pressure of the gas.

F_{Gas} stands for the percentage of the gas.

P_{amb} stands for the ambient pressure.

F stands for fraction (proportion).

amb stands for ambient (surroundings)

P stands for pressure.

This formula is a help to obtain the single pressures. It states that you must either multiply or divide each factor to arrive at the value you are looking for.

Partial pressure: F_{gas} multiplicated with P_{amb} is P_{gas}

Ambient pressure: P_{gas} divided by F_{gas} is P_{amb}

Gas proportion: P_{gas} divided by P_{amb} is F_{gas}

If you now hide the number you are looking for, the calculation with the open numbers (times or divide) shows the result. Of course, you only have to use this procedure if you want to mix your own gases and go diving with them. If you dive with Nitrox at any dive center in the world, it is important to analyze the content of your own scuba tank before the dive. And if the oxygen content is not right, get another scuba tank. But then check the oxygen content again, please.

Now a few sample calculations for understanding.

1. The maximum oxygen partial pressure should be 1.4 bar. The mixture has a 28% oxygen content. What maximum ambient pressure is allowed?

We are looking for P_{amb}

Ambient pressure: P_{gas} divided by F_{gas} is P_{amb}

$$\frac{1,4 \text{ bar}}{0,28} = 5 \text{ bar}$$

5 bar prevail in a water depth of 40 meters!

2. Same values but now we are looking for the oxygen content.

Gas proportion: P_{gas} divided by P_{amb} is F_{gas}

$$\frac{1,4 \text{ bar}}{5 \text{ bar}} = 0,28 \text{ is 28\% oxygen proportion.}$$

3. Again the same values but now we want to calculate the partial pressure.

Partial pressure: F_{gas} times P_{amb} is P_{gas}

0,28 x 5 bar = 1,4 bar

And now you can, if you like, calculate all the necessary values.

MOD

stands for Maximum Operating Depth and indicates the maximum permitted depth with a specific mixture.

In order to calculate the MOD, we first need the

MOP

MOP stands for Maximum Operating Pressure and indicates the maximum permitted ambient pressure.

We calculate a test dive with 36% oxygen content.

Maximum oxygen partial pressure may be 1.4 bar, which we have now internalized.

36% oxygen content is also given.

$$\frac{1,4 \text{ bar}}{0,36} = 3,89 \text{ bar}$$

Thus 3,89 bar is the **MOP**

Since we know that we always have to subtract 1 bar surface pressure to get to the pure water pressure, we now subtract 1 bar from the 3.89 bar and thus get 2.89 bar.

We have 2.89 bar water pressure at a depth of 28.9 meters. Thus, 28.9 meters is our MOD. We should not dive deeper with this mixture.

We make sure by looking at page 153 and find everything fits. Correctly calculated.

And now just stick to the depth specifications on page 153 and stay within no-stop times, then you're on the safe side. And even if you have to make a decompression stop, you're still on the safe side when diving with Nitrox. Since you have less nitrogen in your breathing gas mixture but still decompress according to a table (e. g. Deko 2000), which assumes a higher nitrogen content.

Advantage of Nitrox

Theoretically, you could, if you have practiced the calculations, extend the no-stop times in a specific depth (keyword EAD). But that makes little sense in normal diving on holiday, because then you increase the risk of a decompression accident and lose the advantage of Nitrox. Namely the greater security against a decompression accident.

The same applies to the decompression times, which you could theoretically shorten if you perform the corresponding calculations.

The reduced nitrogen content of your breathing air reduces the risk of microbubble formation. Microbubbles, as the name implies, are microscopic gas bubbles that actually form on each dive, but do not cause damage if we stay within the no-stop time or decompress properly.

Due to the lower nitrogen content of the breathing air, of course, the burden on the body by the nitrogen is lower. Thus, the risk of a depth intoxication is, at least theoretically, reduced and also the risk of suffering a decompression accident.

In addition, there are divers who feel fresher and less exhausted after diving with Nitrox. Often only after the second dive.

For divers which make several dives a day, instructor assistants, dive guides and instructors, Nitrox is the mixture of choice.

Disadvantage of Nitrox

What has advantages, experience has shown, has unfortunately also disadvantages. Of course this also applies to Nitrox.

- Due to the increased oxygen content, the burden on the central nervous system of humans is also higher. However, if you strictly adhere to the depth limits and do not exceed them, nothing can happen to you. But it must not be concealed that there are people who nevertheless get problems with the increased oxygen content.

This is very seldom and you can also get used to the increased oxygen content. Just as Reinhold Meßmer got used to climbing Mount Everest without oxygen. However, if you feel unwell when diving with Nitrox, leave the water and dive furthermore with air. If you want to get to the root of the problem, you can go to a specialist and undergo an oxygen tolerance test. Unfortunately, the health insurance does not pay this test. But as I said, this happens only very rarely.

- With Nitrox you should not dive as deep as with normal air. See page 153.

- The equipment, especially the valves and the regulators, must be "oxygen clean", meaning that special seals must be used and no grease must be used. Oxygen and grease (silicone grease etc.) are natural enemies and when they come together it can get pretty loud.

- Oxygen promotes combustion (oxidation).

- The filling station must be specially designed.

- The filling costs are increased, at least for the base operator.

- The dive must be planned and calculated very carefully. The MOD must be adhered to. Even though my often quoted golden treasure is lying beneath you, under no circumstances should you dive deeper than the MOD allows.

- With your special nitrox tank, you must not go to a "normal" air filling station, as you get there no absolutely grease and oil-free air. Even if the amount of oil in the air mixture is extremely low, these small proportions may accumulate over time and explode when they get in touch with pure oxygen.

- It must / should always be dived with a Nitrox suitable diving computer and the maximum oxygen partial pressure (1.4 bar) and the mixture used (EAN 32 or EAN 36) must always be entered and checked prior to the dive.

- Some countries in the EU require a special regulator thread (M26 x 2).

- The utensils used (regulator, diving equipment, inflators) must be checked and cleaned once a year to detect and eliminate any accumulation of grease or oil.

- Generally you can go diving with nitrox in mountain lakes (Altitude Diving, i.e. at altitudes ≥ 300 meters) too. However, as there are no validated data available, you should dive as if you were using normal air (21% oxygen).

The US National Oceanic and Atmospheric Administration (NOAA) states that we can use our normal equipment, with no modification, up to 40% oxygen in the breathing gas mixture. This directive has been used in the United States for many years and has proven itself. In Europe, however, there are also other opinions. In Germany, for example, any gas mixture which has more than 21% oxygen content, is to treat as pure oxygen. However, it should not be concealed that during the filling and mixing process, when filling by partial pressure method, explosions are possible if oils and / or grease that are not oxygen-compatible are located on or in the scuba tank. The partial pressure filling method uses pure oxygen (100%). Therefore, only oxygen-clean diving tanks may be filled according to this method.

Medical aspects of diving with Nitrox

What happens if we exceed the MOD (Maximum Operating Depth) when using a specific gas mixture?

When we exceed this depth limit, a **hyperoxia** occurs. Hyper means too much and Oxie stands for oxygen. This simply means too much oxygen. In this case, too much oxygen pressure. As already mentioned, we should avoid an oxygen partial pressure of over 1.4 bar. But, as is sometimes the case, the risk attracts us and we want to see where our limits are. That is completely human and therefore often stupid.

Paul Bert found out as early as 1878 that oxygen, inhaled under increased pressure, has a toxic effect on the body. This increased oxygen partial pressure has a narcotic effect on the central nervous system (CNS). This effect is named in honor of Mr. Bert also Paul-Bert effect.

What exactly happens to us when we inhale the oxygen with a partial pressure of more than 1.4 bar?

At the same time, two things happen to our body.

Symptom No. 1

Central nervous system (CNS) disorders, Paul-Bert effect

Neurotoxic effects of hyperoxia

- Muscle tremors, twitching and cramps

- Eye disorders, blurred vision

- Malaise, nausea

- Hallucinations, confusion, metallic taste

- Inner ear disorders, ear noises

If you notice it by yourself, it is necessary to ascend several meters immediately. It is best to leave the water after the safety stop (3 minutes at 5 meters) has been carried out. Conclusion: Be sure to always and especially when using Nitrox, **never exceed** the 1.4 bar oxygen partial pressure.

The general oxygen tolerance limit in humans is an oxygen partial pressure of 1.82 bar and an exposure time of one minute. For us recreational divers that is less important but the colleague who operates the pressure chamber, if we have miscalculated, should know that. Pressure chamber treatments typically begin with 100% oxygen at 18 meters of simulated water depth. The patient is lying and gets 20 minutes of pure oxygen and then follows a 5 minute oxygen break. The problem with the seizures is tolerated, because usually the patient has bigger problems than a seizure in

164

a controlled environment. (Note from the pressure chamber operator).

Symptom No. 2

The lung effect, also called Lorraine-Smith effect.

Oxygen is a very reactive gas and has the property to damage the alveoli under increased pressure and long exposure time. Symptoms of this oxygen overpressure are:

- Damage to the lung tissue (alveoli)

- Irritation of the pharyngeal mucosa

- Burning and stinging in the eyes

- Unstoppable cough

- Possibly unconsciousness

- Hypoxia (lack of oxygen) due to damage to the alveoli

In the worst case, the increased oxygen partial pressure can cause bursting of the alveoli. This reduces the lung surface, which is essential for gas exchange, resulting in reduced oxygen uptake and reduced carbon dioxide release. Ignoring this "ability" of oxygen, it can come to the point where the effective lung surface is so greatly reduced that the affected person suffocates.

And if you now believe that you can dive indefinitely as long as you don't exceed the 1.4 bar oxygen partial pressure, you are unfortunately wrong. At least from a medical point of view. But the time you can stay under this pressure without taking damage is 153 minutes, and before that happens you are freezing or thirsty. Keyword OTU.

What means OTU?

The oxygen tolerance unit, abbreviated OTU, is a value indicating the permissible oxygen units.

A unit is composed of the amount (partial pressure) of the oxygen in the breathing gas mixture and the pressure (ambient pressure) at which we inhale this mixture. Both values add up to the OTU and show us, according to the table, how many units we can consume safely.

For example, you can breathe in a breathing gas mixture with a low oxygen content and at a low ambient pressure over a long period of time without being harmed. You can already tell by the fact that we can breathe in the 21% oxygen contained in our normal breathing air for a very long time, a whole life long, without suffering excessive damage.

But if we now increase the amount of oxygen in our breathing air, let's say to 50%, then the time we can breathe in that mixture without suffering any damage is considerably shorter. If we now increase the proportion of oxygen to 100% and breathe in this gas under normal pressure, it comes and there are the physicians seemingly not really agree, after several days to a damage of the body.

If we now increase the pressure, we multiply the damaging potential of oxygen by compressing it. For example by diving to a certain depth, the time that we can inhale this breathing gas safely reduces to a few hours or even minutes.

Note: The higher the proportion of oxygen in the breathing gas mixture and the higher the pressure at which we inhale this mixture, the more damaging this gas is to our body.

In the following table (page 168) you can see which oxygen partial pressure (PO2 or ppO2) you can breathe safely and how long you can. IDA recommends always staying under 700 units (OTU) per day.

We will come to the CNS later, but again only 80% of the allowed oxygen uptake should be used to avoid damage. Now, if you go on a longer dive holiday and dive with Nitrox daily, you must remember that the harmful effects of oxygen breathed under increased pressure **add up**. For this reason, the daily tolerable OTU value is reduced every day. From the 7th day you should absolutely take one day diving break. In addition, you should have at least one hour of surface break between each dive a day. If you are still allowed to consume 700 OTUs on the first day, the maximum tolerable OTU value for the following days is reduced as follows:

2. Day 620 OTU

3. Day 525 OTU

4. Day 460 OTU

5. Day 420 OTU

6. Day 380 OTU

7. Day 300 OTU

Diving break

(do something nice with the family) :-)

IDA CNS/OTU charts based on NOAA

PO$_2$ (bar)	OTU's (1/ min)	CNS %/ min	dive time max. (min)	PO$_2$ (bar)	OTU's (1/ min)	CNS %/ min	dive time max. (min)
0,50	0,00	0,00	>	1,22	1,35	0,48	208
0,60	0,26	0,14	714	1,24	1,38	0,51	196
0,64	0,35	0,15	666	1,26	1,42	0,52	192
0,66	0,39	0,16	625	1,28	1,45	0,54	185
0,68	0,43	0,17	588	1,30	1,48	0,56	178
0,70	0,47	0,18	555	1,32	1,51	0,57	175
0,74	0,54	0,19	526	1,34	1,54	0,60	166
0,76	0,58	0,20	500	1,36	1,57	0,62	161
0,78	0,62	0,21	476	1,38	1,60	0,63	158
0,80	0,65	0,22	454	1,40	1,63	0,65	153
0,82	0,69	0,23	434	1,42	1,66	0,68	147
0,84	0,73	0,24	416	1,44	1,69	0,71	140
0,86	0,76	0,25	400	1,46	1,72	0,74	135
0,88	0,80	0,26	384	1,48	1,75	0,78	128
0,90	0,83	0,28	357	1,50	1,78	0,83	120
0,92	0,87	0,29	344	1,52	1,81	0,93	107
0,94	0,90	0,30	333	1,54	1,84	1,04	96
0,96	0,93	0,31	322	1,56	1,87	1,19	84
0,98	0.97	0,32	312	1,58	1,89	1,47	68
1,00	1,00	0,33	303	1,60	1,92	2,22	45
1,02	1,03	0,35	285	1,62	1,95	5,00	20
1,04	1,07	0,36	277	1,65	2,00	6,25	16
1,06	1,10	0,38	263	1,67	2,03	7,69	13
1,08	1,13	0,40	250	1,70	2,07	10,00	10
1,10	1,16	0,42	238	1,72	2,10	12,50	8
1,12	1,20	0,43	232	1,74	2,13	20,00	5
1,14	1,23	0,43	232	1,76	2,15	25,00	4
1,16	1,26	0,44	227	1,78	2,18	33,33	3
1,18	1,29	0,46	217	1,80	2,21	50,00	2
1,20	1,32	0,47	212	1,82	2,24	100,00	1

Example

Oxygen partial pressure 1.4 bar.

You now look in the table on the left column and look for the 1.4 bar PO2. These can be found in the right-hand block of the table in the eleventh row. To the right you will find the 1.63, which gives the OTU value per minute at this partial pressure. At the far right of this line, you will find the time in minutes that you can dive with this partial oxygen pressure, namely 153 minutes. These 153 minutes indicate the maximum time you can dive at this oxygen partial pressure during a dive.

If you stay under water at this oxygen partial pressure (1.4 bar) for just 60 minutes, multiply the 1.63 with the dive time in minutes

60 x 1.63 and then you come to the OTU value 97.8

This puts you well below the maximum allowable 700 OTUs per day that IDA recommends.

Therefore, you can, without any problems, make another dive with this partial pressure on the same day. Especially since the surface break has another positive effect on the recovery of the body.

If you now reduce the oxygen partial pressure, you will also get significantly less OTU's per minute.

Example

Gas Mixture Nitrox 34

Oxygen partial pressure on the surface is 0.34 bar.

Diving depth max. 20 meters is equal to 3 bar ambient pressure.

Dive time should be 60 minutes.

0.34 bar PO_2 x 3 bar corresponds to an oxygen partial pressure of 1.02 bar. A look at the table shows an OTU of 1.03. In the right column we can now read the maximum possible dive time of 285 minutes.

For this dive, we now have to count 1.03 times the dive time in minutes, so 60 minutes.

1,03 x 60 is 61,8 OTU

So here are only 61.8 OTU's to be counted.

Based on these calculations, you can see that you can expect to remain submerged for hours on end with a Nitrox mix with 32 or 36% oxygen, without harming your body.

But even if the maximum value of ≤ 700 OTU's per day is barely reached in practice, you should never lose sight of this value for the sake of your health.

Maximalgrenzen O$_2$-Exposition

O$_2$-Partialdruck (bar)	1.6	1.5	1.4	1.3	1.2	1.1	1.0	0.9	0.8	0.7	0.6
Einzelexposition (min)	45	120	150	170	210	230	300	350	450	550	710
24-h-Exposition (min)	150	180	180	210	240	270	300	350	450	550	710

From the above table it can be seen at which oxygen partial pressure (O$_2$ –Partialdruck) you can stay for how long without causing damage to your body.

Example: Oxygen partial pressure 1.4 bar.

A dive can last a maximum of 150 minutes (Einzelexposition). Within 24 hours you can breathe a partial pressure of oxygen of 1.4 bar for a maximum of 180 minutes (24 h Exposition). For example 3 dives to 60 minutes.

Oxygen breathed under increased pressure also has a negative effect on our central nervous system (CNS), which we must also consider. You will also find a value in the table on page 168, more precisely in the third column. This value indicates how much % of the health tolerated dose of hyperbaric oxygen, i.e. oxygen with an increased partial pressure (gas pressure), you can inhale per minute, without causing damage to your central nervous system.

Example

Oxygen partial pressure 1.4 bar

You look again in the left column and look there the 1.4 bar oxygen partial pressure. Then move to the right in the same row until you have landed in the third column with the CNS% / minute.

There you will find the number 0.65. Please remember.

Now you dive and make your dive at an oxygen partial pressure of 1.4 bar and stay under water for 60 minutes. You know that according to the table, that you dive under this pressure, you must multiply the value of 0.65 with every minute. And you know that you should not get over 80% per dive day.

Calculation: 60 minutes x 0.65 = 39 %

Example

Nitrox 32

But now you dive not with an oxygen partial pressure of 1.4 bar but use Nitrox 32, with an oxygen content of 32% and do not go so low that the 1.4 bar oxygen partial pressure will be reached.

Let's assume you go to a maximum depth of 20 meters and stay there for 60 minutes.

With Nitrox 32 you have an oxygen partial pressure of 3 bar x 0.32 bar = 0.96 bar at a depth of 20 meters

So we look at 0.96 bar in the table and find there 0.32 below CNS% / minute.

So now we multiply the 60 minutes with the value 0.32 and then we get 19.2 as a result.

Thus, with this dive, we achieved 19.2% of the maximum oxygen uptake for this dive day.

In theory, we could perform 4 dives of this quality in one day, without fear of damage to the central nervous system.

By maintaining longer surface pauses (SFP), you can also reduce the strain on your CNS.

Reduction factor during surface break

SFP (minute)	0	30	60	90	120	150	180	240	300	360	540
CNS factor	1	0,8	0,63	0,5	0,4	0,31	0,25	0,16	0,1	0,06	0

To do this, take the time of your surface break, say 2 hours (120 minutes), and then look at the factor below, which is 0.4. According to the dive above, you had a CNS load of 19.2% because of the previous dive. Now multiply this 19.2% by 0.4 and then you have 7.68% as a result. Thus, you reduced your CNS load from 19.2% to 7.68% because you had 2 hours surface break. This affects the next dive, since up to 80% of the total oxygen intake per day is allowed. But do not go too far to the limits and take good care of yourself.

Here's a tip for those who do not want to look on tables and calculate everything. Either stay with your Instructor, because these professionals know exactly how long and how deep you can dive without a risk of damage. Or invest in a good dive computer. There, you enter only the 1.4 bar oxygen partial pressure limit, if this is not already done ex works and also type in the oxygen content of your gas mixture. The rest is then taken over by the computer and it also makes sure that nothing happens to you. Provided you always keep an eye on your computer's displays and warnings. If your computer should fail during the dive, you should immediately go to a water depth of 5 meters and stay there for at least 5 minutes before leaving the water. A second dive computer (redundancy) would also be a solution if you want to be completely safe.

Let us now turn to another advantage of Nitrox that is particularly appreciated by those who go diving long and / or often. Among these people are the very ambitious scuba divers as well as instructors, research divers and professional divers.

The keyword is EAD. EAD stands for **equivalent air depth**. If we calculate the EAD before each dive, we can, if necessary, decompress according to the deco table for air (Deko 2000). Then, however, the positive effect of reducing the risk of a decompression accident is lost.

The beauty of Nitrox is that the nitrogen content of our gas mixture is lower than in normal breathing air. Thus, we also absorb less nitrogen and have an advantage in relation to the no-stop time and also during any necessary decompression stops.

If we have less nitrogen in our breathing gas mixture, we reach the "critical" nitrogen partial pressure later than the compressed air diver.

When diving with Nitrox, the EAD is **always** less than the actual depth. Thus, we **always** have a longer no-stop time.

Example

Nitrox 32

32 % Oxygen and 68 % Nitrogen.

Actual diving depth 20 meters, i.e. 3 bar.

Now we have to determine the ratio of nitrogen content to each other, as these significantly influence the decompression.

We call this ratio the Equivalent Factor (EF).

$$EF = \frac{\text{Nitrogen partial pressure } \textbf{Nitrox}}{\text{Nitrogen partial pressure } \textbf{Air}} = \frac{0.68}{0.79} = 0.86$$

The EF is 0.86

We now multiply this value by the pressure in the actual diving depth and obtain the equivalent air pressure (EAP).

0.86 x 3 bar = 2.58 bar (EAP)

2.58 bar ambient pressure results in a water depth of 15.8 meters (EAD).

Now let's have a look at the Deko 2000 and see there, in the column up to 18 meters, a no-stop time of 45 minutes. If we had done this dive with compressed air, we would have to use the column up to 21 meters and would have a no-stop time of only 31 minutes.

So by using Nitrox 32 we have a no-stop time that is 14 minutes longer.

Now we take a Nitrox 40 mixture for the same dive. EF calculation as before (take a look at the page before).

EF = 0.76

0.76 x 3 bar = 2.28 bar (EAP)

Now EAD is 12.8 Meter

Thus, we look in the table in the column to 15 meters and get there a no-stop time of 72 minutes.

Compared to pure breathing air, we have a time advantage of 41 minutes.

Whether that is suitable for you or not, you have to decide by yourself. However, you should always, in order not to let it come to accidents, carry a Nitrox suitable dive computer. Nobody stops you from calculating your dives and write notes on your wetnotes (example next page). Today's dive computers are no longer prone to mistakes, but if it does happen, you'll be prepared if you've thought about it before.

Wetnotes to be fixed

on the forearm.

Made of plastic and rewritable.

Technology and equipment!

In the Nitrox mixture, the oxygen content is, as a rule, significantly higher than in normal breathing air.

Oxygen is an oxidizing gas and it promotes combustion, so does Nitrox.

Nitrox mixtures may only be manufactured by qualified persons using special material (compressors and overflow tanks or membrane systems). Never mix your own gas mixtures if you have not been trained for it before. IDA offers the course Gasblender. The higher the oxygen partial pressure in the mixture, the more violent is the reaction in case of burns or explosions, since oxygen is a strongly oxidizing gas.

In Germany it is regulated by law that a gas mixture containing more than 21% oxygen should be treated like pure oxygen. In other countries, this rule is not so strict.

From these specifications results that our diving equipment must be **Oxygen suitable**.

Equipment parts are suitable if they have a general oxygen compatibility and are oxygen-clean.

A normal diving equipment must be specially cleaned before use with Nitrox. This process is called "cleaning" in common usage. This cleaning should only be carried out by **specialized personnel**, since all parts of the equipment that come into contact with the increased oxygen content or the pure oxygen must be absolutely clean. After cleaning, the specialist will attach a tank sticker (Nitrox Clean or Oxygen Clean), which confirms the suitability of the diving equipment for Nitrox. The same applies to the regulator and (if we take it strictly) the lifejacket and also the drysuit. So any part that comes directly into contact with the gas and could possibly have oil or grease residues. Before you bring your equipment to "cleaning", make sure that the manufacturer of your equipment has also released them for use with Nitrox. That's not always the case. Some manufacturers of regulators offer corresponding Nitrox regulators "ex works" and also the corresponding diving equipment can be purchased "ex works". Then the first "cleaning" treatment is omitted.

Not compatible with oxygen:

Titanium alloys or titanium, zinc, neoprene, lubricants (oil, grease, silicone)

Oxygen compatible are:

Copper, Teflon, Viton O-rings, special lubricants (Voltalef, Krytox, Fonblin, Tribolub)

Oxygen-clean is our material when it is absolutely clean and free from contamination, especially in the high-pressure area (tank, valve, regulator). Contaminants are oils and greases (exception lubricants, see above), rust particles, soaps and detergents of all kinds.

Tanks, regulators and valves should be inspected once a year by a dealer. This inspection should be confirmed by the dealer with a sticker (Nitrox Clean or Oxygen Clean). The tank should generally be marked with a special sticker or paintwork as a tank for Nitrox so that it will not be accidentally filled at a normal air filling station. The paintwork or the sticker should be large, best around the tank, so it can't not be overlooked.

Example

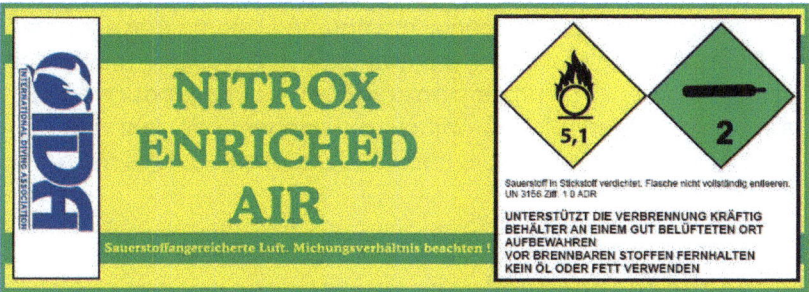

The regulator connection (thread), which is 5/8 inch when using normal breathing air, must be M26 x 2 when using Nitrox to avoid confusion. So a special cylinder valve is needed and the regulator must, after cleaning, also get a special handwheel to the tank connection. However, it is best if you simply get a completely new Nitrox-compatible equipment. That puts you on the safe side.

Note: A filling station for Nitrox offers an oil-free filling, as otherwise explosions may occur. This means that any "non-nitrox-compatible diving tank" can be filled there with normal compressed air. Otherwise, a nitrox tank, which is used exclusively for the use of enriched gases, should never be filled at a normal air filling station, as there no oil-free fillings can be guaranteed. If the tank filled there should later be filled with Nitrox and it is not previously made clean for oxygen use, an explosion can occur. Should it nevertheless happen, the diving equipment must be cleaned again by a specialist before it can be filled with Nitrox.

There are two ways to fill nitrox into a scuba tank. In the so-called partial pressure method, pure oxygen is first filled into the diving tank and then filled up with normal air. Thereafter, the mixture must rest for at least 12 hours to ensure optimal mixing. Working with pure oxygen is very dangerous because oxygen is a very reactive gas and many a compressor shed has lost its roof due to inappropriate handling of pure oxygen. If not worse has happened.

Less dangerous and therefore also "state of the art" in the meantime, is the use of special membrane systems that are able to filter the nitrogen out of the breathing air. With these membrane systems today all common nitrox mixtures can be produced up to an oxygen content of 40%, without the danger of dealing with pure oxygen. The mixture is then ready to use and does not have to rest.

Membrane system

Nitrox is made by filtering out nitrogen.

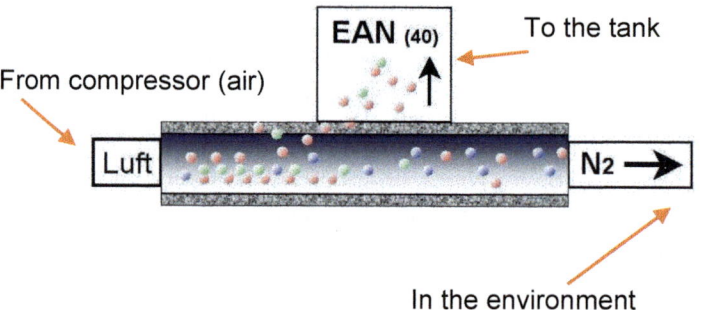

Practice

Before the dive, the following should be noted:

- Is my partner diving with Nitrox? Which mixture does he use and which depth (MOD) can we visit to a maximum?

- If my partner dives with normal air (Nitrox 21 :-), I have to point out to him that I dive with Nitrox and tell him the consequences that result. (Maximum depth, advantages with a possible decompression (EAD), longer bottom times, possible benefits in the case of depth intoxication).

- Gas mixture must be analyzed immediately before the dive and the oxygen content must be noted on the tank label. As an individual and inexpensive tank sticker, it is not meant the nitrox sticker from any of the previous pages, usually a strip of tape is used. The following must be noted on this sticker: percent oxygen percentage, maximum permissible depth with this mixture, name of testing person and date of test. For legal reasons, these data must also be noted in a special filling logbook.

You can do it like this!

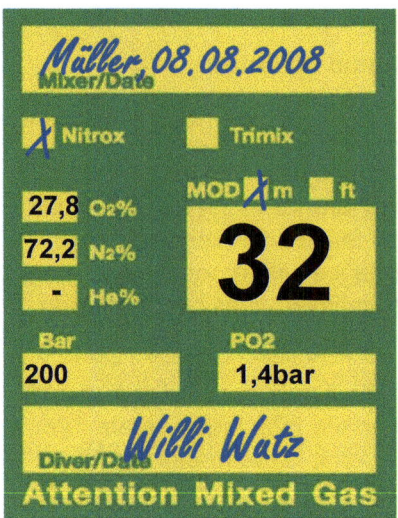

That's better! 😊

- The dive computer must be set to the correct mixture.

- The dive computer must be set to the maximum oxygen partial pressure of 1.4 bar. Often this setting is already adjusted ex works.

During the dive, the following should be noted:

- MOD (max. diving depth) must not be exceeded.

- Control of the partner for possible oxygen intolerance, if he/she dives with Nitrox.

- Self-check for possible oxygen intolerance.

- If your instructor has placed a safety deco tank at a depth of 5 meters in order to allow the divers who run out of air the safety decompression stop, pay attention to the contents of this tank. The breathing gas in this tank should always have the same composition as the breathing gas you use. If this diving tank has a content of more oxygen than your own diving equipment, this is relatively uncritical, since this does not affect the subsequent dives and if anything, then only positive, in terms of decompression. The additional oxygen effect (OTU / CNS) is negligible at a deco stop of a few minutes. However, if there is a gas mixture in this decompression tank which has a lower oxygen content than your own breathing gas mixture, this is not uncritical. Because your dive computer calculates for this dive and also for possible repetitive dives with the previously entered values, so for example with Nitrox 36. However, perhaps is Nitrox 21, which is compressed air, in the safety deco tank, which can have a negative effect on your residual nitrogen saturation in the body, since you are not breathing 64% nitrogen (Nitrox 36) but 79% nitrogen (compressed air). Many dive computers have the ability to set a second breathing gas and then consider that gas for decompression and subsequent dives. If you perform such dives frequently, with safety stops on 5 meters, you buy such a dive computer and learn to handle it properly and make the correct settings.

After the dive, the following should be noted:

- Write the dive with all information in your logbook.

- Write the residual pressure of the tank on the control sheet and the tank sticker (e.g. tape).

- The person refilling the diving tank must attach a new sticker with the corresponding data. Percent of oxygen percentage, maximum permissible depth with this mixture, name of the examiner and the date of the test.

Always follow the guidelines and laws that apply in the country in which you dive. There are for example, countries in which a freshly mixed nitrox mixture may be used for a maximum of 30 days or countries in which the color coding of the diving tanks is different. If you are unsure, ask your base leader or your instructor.

If you dive with Nitrox frequently, even at home, you should get your own analyzer. Then you can ensure that you always have exactly the mixture in your scuba, which should be in it. Observe the specifications of the manufacturer and bear in mind that the oxygen sensor also has to be replaced from time to time (with modern devices, the sensor will last about 2 to 3 years). Always keep in mind that the correct amount of oxygen in your breathing gas mixture is very important because your life depends on it. If possible, check your gas mixture more than once and, if possible, do not let your diving equipment out of sight after checking it.

Keep a record of your nitrox dives so you and the others can comprehend what happened to you in the event of an accident and why the accident might have happened.

IDA Nitroxplaner

Name, first name:	
Date, time:	
Place	
Diving site:	
Name, first name of the partner	
Name, first name of the partner	

Planning data		
CNS O_2 % before the dive	CNS O_2 %	
Repetitive group and surface break	RG:	SB
Gas mixture (EAN % O_2)	fO_2 :	fN_2 :
O_2 – Proportion measured	O_2 % :	Date
Gas in stock barL = P x V (Note the reserve)		
O_2- partial pressure(max. 1,4 bar) $pPO_2 = fO_2$ x P		
Max. depth (MOD in m) MOP = pPO_2 / fO_2		

Dive planning		Analysis
	Planned	Carried out
Depth and ambient pressure		
Equivalent depht (EAD) EAP = PpN_2 / 0,79 bar		
Bottom time		
Dekoplan (Deko 2000 _____ over sea level		
Safety stop 3 min. / 5 meter		
Total diving time		
Gas consuption (barl)		
CNS O_2 % - Total (IDA CNS table)		
CNS O_2 % - Increase		
Signature		

Many dive centers that offer EAN gas mixtures also carry a so-called fill log, which contains special data pertaining to the filled diving tank. Therefore, if you pick up a freshly filled diving tank there, with the gas mixture corresponding to your diving depth, you often have to acknowledge receipt. This signature is primarily for the safety of the person who has filled your diving tank and secondarily for your own safety. Since on the control sheet also the serial number or an inventory number of the diving tank, given by the diving base, is written. This is to prevent accidental interchange of the diving tank. Check both this number and the contents of the diving tank (gas analysis) before signing the filling sheet. On the following page you will find an IDA fill sheet design.

I, _____, hereby certify

First name, name

that I have the diving tank with the number: _____

Serial or inventory number of the tank

on _____ subjected to a gas analysis.

date

I received the tank on _____ from

date

_____

Name of the diving base / the instructor

and measured an oxygen content of _____ %

The gas mixture was made by _____

Name of the gasblender

and labeled as_____

Oxygen content (e.g. Nitrox 32)

This means that I can dive with this breathing gas mixture to a

maximum depth of _____meter.

The filling pressure of the tank is_____ bar.

_____   _____

First name and name of the diver   Signature of the diver

So, that was it for now. Now you can get started and gain experience. Take care of yourself and have the courage to even break off a dive or not even go into the water, if you do not feel well. A good diving partner understands this. Safety is the most important thing. And keep in mind, a good diving partner is the best life insurance you can have but

"No buddy is perfect"

and so even your diving partner can make mistakes. So take care of yourself and have a lot of fantastic dives.

Note of thanks!

Hereby I would like to thank the following friends for having read my treatise several times, so that I can be sure that I have not told you nonsense. I especially thank my darling Karen for accepting my intuitive punctuation and guiding her into appropriate paths. The comma has always been my friend, or alternatively my enemy. ☺ My problem is that the English punctuation does not match the German one at all. I'm very sorry, please excuse it. I'm a diving instructor and a Radar electronics technician not a grammar teacher.

Karen Fink, IDA diver and model for the UW-signs.

Horst Habermehl, President of the International Diving Association - IDA -, Instructor Examiner and former seal of the German Navy.

Thomas Freudenberg, chairman of the Instructor Examination board of IDA, Master Chief Officer and Diving Instructor of the German Navy, Professional Diver and member of the German Industry and commerce chamber for professional divers.

Markus Schneider, IDA Diving Instructor and base leader

Thomas Burkhardt, former chief of the IDA Instructor Examination board.

Marcus Reiner, IDA Diver and model for the „special" UW-sign.

Jens Dawurske, IDA Diver and a very great help with the translation. Thanks a lot my friend, if you had not noticed, that I had forgotten to translate some sentences, I would certainly have had trouble with some of my English speaking dive mates. 😊

What is IDA - International Diving Association?

IDA is an international association of diving instructors and member of CMAS Germany and R.S.T.C. (Recreational Scuba Training Council). IDA trains divers and diving instructors worldwide.

Scuba is the shortcut for „**S**elf **C**ontained **U**nderwater **B**reathing **A**pparatus"!

IDA was founded in 1996 and since then has been very successful in trying to reconcile the American "Easy Diving" with the "European (German) will to perfection". This does not always work 100%. Nonetheless, IDA has managed to license nearly 1600 IDA Instructors around the world who are training and checking divers under the IDA guidelines. IDA is a partner of CMAS Germany and a member of R.S.T.C. Both organizations cover about 90% of the international diving education market with their member associations and ensure that you can safely learn and enjoy diving for years to come.

6. Appendix

Here is an excerpt from the recommendation for the dive group compilation of the IDA:

Only the allowed pairings are mentioned.

Open Water Diver or Diver *

and

Advanced Open Water Diver	to 18 meter depth
Diver**	to 20 meter depth
Master Scuba Diver	to 20 meter depth
from Diver *** and higher	to 40 meter depth

Junior Open Water Diver

and

Diveguide and / or higher (Assistant Instructor or Instructor) to 8 meter depth.

Generally, according to IDA recommendation and age, the following maximum depths apply:

8 – 10 years	5 meter
10 – 12 years	5 meter
12 – 16 years	12 meter
16 – 18 years	25 meter
From 18 years	40 meter

Glossary:

50 bar rule

50 bar residual pressure is the safety reserve and should not be part of the diving calculation

40m

Depth limit for Recreational diver

No-stop-time dives

IDA recommend no-stop-time dives

Descent speed / rate

Max. 30 m / min.

Safety stop

3 minutes at 5 meters at every dive which leads deeper than 5 meters

Surface pause

IDA recommend a surface pause of at least 2 hours between two dives

Repetitive dives

IDA recommend to make not more than two dives a day

Order

IDA recommend to make the deepest dive at first

Compression phase

Pressure increase during descent

Isopression phase

Constant pressure, the diver remains at a constant depth

Variopression phase

Changing ambient pressure corresponds to the real one

dive profile

Decompression phase

Pressure decrease on ascent

No-stop-time

The time you can stay in a certain depth of water

in which a decompression stop is not necessary

Bottom time

The time from the descent to the beginning of the ascent

Ascent time

The time, without decompression pauses, which is needed for the pure ascent

BMV Breath minute volume

The amount of air you need to breathe in a minute, at the surface

Decompression stop

Length of stay at a certain depth level to give the nitrogen the chance to leave the body.

Surface pause

The time between two dives

No Fly Time

The time which should lie between the last dive and a flight, since in the aircraft cabin a reduced air pressure prevails. This reduced cabin pressure can lead in extreme cases to a decompression sickness. This time should, for safety's sake, always be more than 24 hours.

Instructor

Shortcut for diving instructor.

Assistant Instructor

Shortcut for the Assistant of the diving instructor.

Wet recompression

to bring the injured diver back to pressure by diving again.

Share air

Spending air to the partner by using the own regulator

Demonstration of an internationally unusual and very personal underwater hand sign. The dive partner knows the meaning!

You too? ☺

Such hand signals are not uncommon among long-time diving partners. Please remember, however, a third party does not know the meaning! Therefore, before every dive, talk about the UW hand signals. This is recommended especially for new and unknown diving partners.

Statement of health (confidential) © by IDA

Please read all points carefully before signing the form and respond truthfully. Diving is a sport that requires some fitness and good health. The correct answer to these questions is necessary so that your Instructor can see if you are fit for diving. With your signature, you release all employees and also the base or dive school operator (s) from any liability with regard to your state of health. Please note that the IDA recommends that you consult a doctor before the first dive, who will examine your suitability for diving. This form only serves to enable you to dive if you are healthy and no qualified doctor is available. If your health changes during the diving course or during the dives, you are obliged to inform the dive center management immediately. You may only dive if you are healthy or, for example in diabetes, are well adjusted. Persons suffering from heart disease or having severe colds should not dive as well as persons under the influence of drugs, alcohol or other drugs. Even people with extreme overweight or underweight are not suitable for scuba diving unless the doctor decides otherwise. Since diving errors or the handling of the diving equipment can have serious health consequences, you are obliged to dive exclusively under the guidance of a qualified instructor, instructor assistant or dive guide. If you need explanations about the questions below, please contact your instructor before answering the question.

Please answer the following questions in writing with a yes or a no. Your instructor will decide if he will let you dive. If you answer yes to any of these questions, you should consult a doctor before diving.

Medical questionnaire for divers

For the participant:

The following questions should clarify whether you should be examined by a doctor before diving. If you answer one of the questions with a "yes", that does not mean that you are not allowed to dive, but your instructor then decides if you can dive or being send to a doctor for examination. If in doubt, you should consult a doctor. Please take your time answering the questions below.

Do you have or did you had....

Asthma, difficulty breathing or breathing problems during exercise...

Hay fever or bouts of allergies
....

Common colds, sinus problems or bronchitis
....

A lung disease (e.g. pneumothorax)......................................

A lung tear ....

Diseases or operations in the thorax
....

Wear a pacemaker ....

You suffer from mental problems (panic anxiety, fear of

tight spaces)..

You suffer from neurological problems ....

Suffering from a chronic illness ....

You suffer from epilepsy or other seizure disorders ....

You suffer from migraine headaches ....

Have you ever lost consciousness ....

You suffer greatly from motion sickness (car or boat)..................

You suffer from severe diarrhea or dehydration ....

Have you ever had a diving accident (e.g. decompression sickness)...

Do you have problems with physical activity?..............................

Have you had a head injury with unconsciousness in the last 6 years? ....

You suffer from recurrent back problems...................................

Are you (possibly) pregnant ....

Take medications (except malaria prophylaxis and "Pill")..............

Are you a smoker...

Are you in medical care ....

Suffering from elevated cholesterol ....

Have you ever had a heart attack or stroke? ....

Had one of your family members ever had a heart attack or stroke ....

You suffer from diabetes ....

Did you have a surgical procedure on the spine or back? ....

Do you have problems due to surgery on the arms or legs? ....

You suffer from blood pressure disorders or take medication against it ....

Suffer from a blood clot (thrombosis).......................................

Do you suffer from heart disease (angina pectoris or similar)........

Have you ever undergone a surgical procedure on the heart or on a blood vessel? ....

Suffer from dizziness or temporary hearing loss ....

Have you ever been operated on the sinuses? ....

Have you ever been operated on the ears? ....

Do you have problems with the ears ....

Do you have an artificial bowel outlet ....

Take sporty supplements ....

Have you ever been treated for drug addiction (including alcohol)? ....

Have you ever had a soft-tissue fracture (hernias)........................

Do you have problems with the blood ....

Have you undergone surgery within the last 6 weeks ....

Do you have an acute stomach ulcer ....

Do you have problems with pressure equalization? ....

Do you have fever ....

If you currently suffer from the following conditions or illnesses you are not suitable for diving. This also applies if these conditions or illnesses occur during the diving course or vacation.

Pressure equalization problems

Colds, inflammation of the sinuses

Any kind of breathing problems (bronchitis, hay fever)

stomach ulcers

Influence of drugs of any kind (including alcohol)

Pregnancy

Fever

Dizziness

Nausea, seasickness

Diarrhea, dehydration

Migraine or severe headache

Surgical intervention of any kind made within the last 6 weeks

I have the above list today ....

carefully read, understood and noted. So I'm sure I'm fit for diving.
My instructor told me that if I had to answer "yes" to any of the
questions above, I should consult a doctor or seek medical
advice. I declare that I have answered the questionnaire truthfully.

Name, first name:..

Address:..

Date of birth, place of birth:..

Signature:..

Signature of the parent / guardian at minors:................................

Notes: